The Irish Penal System Commission Report
Chairman: Seán MacBride, S.C.
Michael D. Higgins; Senator Gemma Hussey; Michael
Keating, T.D., Dr. Mary McAleese; Patrick McEntee,
S.C.; Dr. Mícheál Mac Gréil, S.J.; Matt Merrigan;
Muireann Ó Briain, B.L.; Una O'Higgins O'Malley

Police Custody and Interrogation
The Barra Ó Briain Committee Report with
Introduction by Kevin T. White, Chairman
Irish Section Amnesty International.

The Right To Take Life: Is
Capital Punishment Justifiable?
By Father Austin Flannery, O.P.

ACKNOWLEDGEMENTS

The publication and wide distribution of this book has been rendered possible by the generous contribution of Dr. Armand Hammer, through the International Peace Bureau.

The Irish Section of Amnesty International, co-publishers of the present book, wish to acknowledge the kind permission of the Controller, Stationery Office, Dublin 4 to reproduct the Ó Briain Committee Report.

CRIME AND PUNISHMENT

edited by Seán Mac Bride, SC

WARD RIVER PRESS
in association with
AMNESTY INTERNATIONAL IRISH SECTION
THE ASSOCIATION OF IRISH JURISTS
THE PRISONERS RIGHTS ORGANISATION

This Collection
First Published 1982 by
Ward River Press Ltd.,
Knocksedan House
Forrest Great
Swords, Co. Dublin, Ireland

ISBN 0 907085 22 9

Cover Design by Steven Hope

Typeset by Lagamage Ltd.
Printed by Cahill Printers Limited,
East Wall Road, Dublin 3.

Contents

PART III
CAPITAL PUNISHMENT

ADVERTISEMENTS

PART I
THE IRISH PENAL SYSTEM

Preface

Neither the moral decadence of the age, nor the climate of violence in which we live could excuse our failure to scrutinise the effectiveness, or otherwise, of our existing penal system.

Leaving aside questions of Christian morality relating to justice and charity, there are many practical reasons which necessitate an objective review of our penal system. Our prison population standing at 1,200 prisoners (with another 1,600 persons on probation) represents a 200% increase in our prison population since 1960. In 1970/1971 we spent £603,028 on our prison system; in 1979 we spent £13,125,906 on our prison system excluding the Curragh Prison and Loughan House. This represents an increase of some 600%! We are planning to spend between ten and twenty million pounds on building additional prisons. Is this vast expenditure serving any useful purpose or is it merely perpetuating a system which breeds recidivism?

In 1978, out of a total expenditure of £9,489,948 on our prison system, only £35,819[1] was spent on prison educational services. Does this represent an acceptable level of educational endeavour necessary for the reintegration into society of the most educationally deprived segment of our population?

What should be the objective of our penal system? Retribution? Punishment? Reform? Rehabilitation? Reintegration into Society? Is custodial incarceration the most effective form of treatment? Would Community Service not be more effective and less wasteful?

---

1. The Minister for Justice (Mr. Gerard Collins, T.D.) points out that, in addition, 48 full time teachers are paid out of the Department of Education vote.

These are some of the questions which the Members of the Commission have sought to examine. It is not claimed that we have found solutions for the many problems that beset our penal system. Many of them arise from structural defects in our society — poverty, unemployment, bad housing, lack of parental responsibility. Others arise from moral, physical or educational handicaps affecting some would-be offenders. Whatever the causes, society has a duty to attempt to rehabilitate and so reintegrate into society those who have transgressed its rules. It should also be remembered that "prevention is better than cure".

We have sought, I trust with objectivity and in a constructive spirit, to analyse the problems involved and suggested some remedies. I hope that the Government will receive this Report as a serious contribution to the solution of what is a grave problem. We had hoped that the Minister for Justice and the Commissioner of the Gárdaí would have been prepared to meet with the Commission to discuss the problems under examination. They both declined. (For correspondence with the Minister and the Commissioner of the Gárdaí, see Appendices 2 and 3).

The Commission held 21 meetings. Over fifty submissions were made to the Commission from experts and other persons in a position to provide relevant information. Most of these submissions were accompanied by written statements. (See Appendix I. for list of written and oral representations). On behalf of the Commission, I would like to express our thanks to all the experts and other persons who gave so much of their time in giving oral testimony or in preparing documentation for the use of the Commission. On behalf of the Commission, it is also my pleasant duty to register our deep appreciation and thanks to the Irish Jesuit Fathers for their generous hospitality and assistance throughout the entire course of our work.

I must also express my sincere thanks to my colleagues in the Commission. They were all busy and responsible citizens in society; in addition to the long hours spent in consultation, many members of the Commission undertook research and the preparation of drafts for the Commission. It is heartening to find concerned citizens coming from different disciplines and professions prepared to undertake, on a voluntary basis, important work on this nature. The sense of social responsibility and willingness to serve the community evidenced by members of the Commission, was a constant source of encouragement throughout the 18 months during which the Commission worked.

I must in particular express my special thanks to Father Mícheál Mac Gréil, S.J. who acted as Editor of the Report, and to Senator Gemma Hussey and Mrs Una O'Higgins O'Malley, who both undertook some of the administrative and research tasks involved. Last but not least I must praise and thank Mrs Maureen Redmond, and Miss Caitriona Lawlor for their excellent secretarial assistance.

Yours sincerely,

Seán MacBride, S.C.
    Chairman,
Commission of Enquiry into
the Irish Penal System

Introduction

No activity of a people so exposes their humanity, their character, their capacity for charity in its most generous dimension, as the treatment they accord persons convicted of crime.

(Ramsey Clark, Former U.S. Attorney General)

The treatment accorded to persons convicted of crime and those in custody prior to their trial for alleged crime in the Republic of Ireland forms the subject matter of this report. The Commission of Enquiry, which has investigated the Irish Penal System and presents its findings, deliberations and recommendations in the following pages, was initiated by the Prisoners' Rights Organisation (PRO) because of the serious need for an examination of our present penal institutions in the context of the developments of modern penology.

The Purpose of the Commission

It must be stated from the beginning that the purpose of the Commission is deliberately constructive and its underlying concern is the promotion of true and just social order in our society. Criticisms of aspects of the current penal system and exposure of practices and structural defects which, in the opinion

13

of the Commission, constitute infringements of human rights and are productive of human and social demoralisation, are made in a constructive sense. Most of these negative and unnecessarily undesirable aspects of the present situation are due more to the inadequacy of the system itself than to any malice of those responsible for its operation. It is hoped, therefore, that the readers of this report will accept it as a genuine contribution by people loyally concerned with the well-being of Irish society and its citizens. It must be stated also that the authors of this report are not motivated or influenced by sectional political loyalties or hostilities.

The Rights of Prisoners

Concern for the rights of prisoners is not only a phenomenon of modern Ireland. It has become a global concern, as evidenced by numerous public enquiries and statements made in recent times by organisations and leaders dedicated to the promotion of a just social order and true human rights. Noteworthy among recent statements are the following: *The Consultation on Christian Concern for Peace* (Baden, Austria, 3.IX.1970), and *The Address of Pope John Paul II to the Irish Bishops* (Dublin, Ireland, 30.IX.1979).

The Baden Consultation, which was organised jointly by the Vatican and the World Council of Churches, drew attention to torture and inhuman treatment of prisoners.

The Christian Churches should be asked to pay special attention to the treatment of all prisoners. National Church authorities and chaplains attached to prisons and other places of detention should familiarise themselves with, and insist upon the application of at least the Standard Minimum Rules for the Treatment of Prisoners approved by the United Nations. Acts of brutality or inhuman treatment of prisoners should always be reported to the highest Church authorities.

(Baden Report)

In his pastoral address to the Irish Bishops, Pope John Paul II reiterated the Baden Reports' concern for prisoners as 'those most needing pastoral care from bishops':

They (the Bishops) should have a special care for those who live on the margin of society. *Among those most needing pastoral care from bishops are prisoners. My dear brothers, do not neglect to provide for their spiritual needs and to concern yourselves also about their material conditions and their families.*

Try to bring the prisoners such spiritual care and guidance as may help to turn them from the ways of violence and crime, and make their detention instead be an occasion of true conversion to Christ and personal experience of love. Have a special care for young offenders. So often their wayward lives are due to society's neglect more than to their own sinfulness. Detention should be especially for them a school of rehabilitation . . .

These extracts from the Baden Consultation and from the recent address of Pope John Paul II point to the immediate moral obligation on Christians to concern themselves with the treatment and rights of those held in penal custody. Such counsel and exhortation should elicit a particular response from

Irish people, the vast majority of whom profess allegiance to the Christian faith.

The Christian Churches are not unique in their appeal for just and humane treatment of prisoners. *The Universal Declaration of Human Rights, The United Nations International Covenant for Civil and Political Rights, The International Committee of the Red Cross, Amnesty International,* and other Human Rights organisations are all adamant in their demands for the protection and promotion of the human rights of prisoners. In view of this impressive body of religious and secular appeals for attention to vigilance and support for worthy standards in dealing with persons in custody, this Commission feels justified in its efforts to investigate and report on the present state of our Irish penal system. The members of the Commission also feel confident that their work will contribute to bringing about the necessary changes in our penal system which will bring it into line with the best standards possible today.

Need for Non-Governmental Commission

The need for this Non-Governmental Commission of Enquiry at the present time is due also to the failure to date on the part of the State to have instituted such an enquiry. It was as a result of such neglect that the PRO invited the members, selected from a wide range of social, political, legal and academic backgrounds*, to constitute themselves as a Commission for the purpose stated. This voluntary team of concerned and experienced citizens, therefore, sees itself as taking a necessary initiative

*See biographical notes on members of the Commission.

in the absence of a public Commission set up by the State. Inevitably, the members are not in a position to have access to all the evidence and documentation which a Government-sponsored Commission would have at its disposal. We failed to persuade the Department of Justice to let us have access to information. Nevertheless, a fairly comprehensive body of evidence and expert opinion has been assembled to substantiate the case made here for reform of the penal system.

Methodology

This report is based on evidence collected from a number of sources. Much reliance has been placed on published literature and research on the various aspects of the penal system. Very valuable and perceptive submissions were made to the Commission at the public hearing in Milltown Park on 6-8th of April 1979, and in private through correspondence and private meetings. The collective experience of the members of the Commission has also been a valuable and critical contribution both in the 'filling of gaps' and in the discernment of what was most reliable in published reports and in submissions.

The Problem of Social Order

Before outlining the scope of this report, it may be worth while to make a few general observations. The Commission does not wish to give the impression that it is unaware of the enormity of the task facing those who are responsible for the maintenance of social order in our society. Coping with crime in society today, whatever its sources, demands a firm and fair response from the authorities. Any solution to the problem of crime calls for action at two levels, namely, the removal of the causes of crime and the restraint and correction of the offender.

The penal system is, of its nature, primarily concerned with the treatment of the offender. The criminal code defines what is criminal behaviour, i.e., activity against public order. Enforcement of the criminal code is the responsibility of the Gardaí and the Department of Justice (which includes civil servants and prison officers). The role of the judiciary and legal profession is the fair application of the criminal law against those deemed to have been in breach of that law.

Objective violation of the criminal law does not, in itself, mean that the offender is guilty of a crime. Motives and circumstances which determine the offender's freedom of action are necessary conditions of criminal guilt. Age, socio-economic background and the cultural environment are particularly relevant determinants of criminal guilt or innocence. They curtail or facilitate the effective freedom of the offender.

The basic norms of society are the specification of its core values. Very often many people do not internalise these norms and values due to inadequacies in their rearing and education. This failure in the transmission to the young of society's values and norms is not infrequently aggravated by the transmission of a different set of values and norms which counter or ignore the accepted values and norms of the dominant group in society. The laws of society are, for the most part, the expression of the values of the dominant group. This inevitably leads to the existence of sub-cultures, i.e., groups whose values and norms are at variance with the dominant group. A high proportion of offenders are likely to come from such sub-cultures. Therefore, the existence of an abnormally high crime rate among members of a particular group may be due more to a failure in education and rearing than to an innate propensity for crime or evil behaviour in the group. This failure is often due to social, cultural, familial and economic deprivation. Such deprivation is ultimately the responsibility of society as a whole.

The situation is made more difficult when there are serious defects in the norms or laws vis-à-vis the cultural values. Very often we suffer from legislative lag. This is very evident in Ireland where many of our criminal laws are obsolete and out of harmony with the modern mentality. When the laws are at variance with the values, the law and the offender suffer. The protection of the basic human rights, however, must always remain the primary purpose of all public law.

Prisoners' Rights Organisation

One result of the lack of research or examination into the Penal System in Ireland (referred to earlier) has been the apathy, or even downright hostility on the part of the public and the political establishment in general to some organisations involved in helping prisoners. Such hostility exists with regard to the Prisoners' Rights Organisation; and indeed, some of its activities have invited the disapproval of the public and the Authorities.

The Members of this Commission were originally approached by the PRO and asked to undertake this work. We did so on the understanding that our work

19

was entirely independent of any group, and since the formation of the Commission, we have not had any meetings with or assistance from the PRO. Therefore, the findings of this Commission must be regarded as being totally independent of any organisation.

We do, however, believe that a need exists for a responsible group to help prisoners both during and after their imprisonment; and we therefore commend the responsible efforts of any group in carrying out this work. In particular, we commend the consistent efforts of the Prisoners' Rights Organisation to focus attention on the need for an Enquiry into the penal system. Their efforts have resulted in this report.

Outline of Report

The Commission was asked to enquire into the present penal system as it is structured and operated in the State. This report contains a systematic examination of our penal system and, by means of a serious and objective analysis of its operation, underlines areas and aspects which are in need of change and modification for the maintenance of true social order and the good of society.

Chapter One traces the historical background to the present system and notes the developments which have led to the state of things today. *Chapter Two* examines the penal system today and tries to identify those areas which are in need of development or discontinuation. *Chapter Three* is concerned with the prison population and presents a fairly comprehensive picture of the occupants of our various penal institutions. One of the striking conclusions of these three chapters is the central place of the custodial and punishment functions and the failure of our prisons to provide for the rehabilitation of the prisoner and the reduction of recidivism. It will also be shown that petty offences are still responsible for a high proportion of imprisoned persons.

Chapter Four addresses itself to the key questions of rehabilitation and recidivism. The Commission draws on well-authenticated evidence from commentators on penal systems outside Ireland to show that the search for alternatives to imprisonment for non-violent and petty offenders should become a top priority. For those who are confined to prison, it will be shown that there is an urgent need for an all-out effort to devise and put into operation ways and means likely to lead to the rehabilitation of the prisoners into society.

In *Chapter Five*, the Commission states its conclusions and recommendations. These include sixty-eight recommendations which vary from suggested structural and procedural changes at the highest level to specific recommendations affecting the care of prisoners, the treatment of juvenile offenders, women's prisons, prevention and rehabilitation, and matters referring to specific prisons.

The report is written and published for the information of the public (in whose name our penal system operates) and for the serious consideration of those with public responsibility for the system. The Commission hopes that its publication will elicit serious debate on our penal system and prepare the way for the necessary changes which are advocated here. If we succeed in these two objectives our work will have been worthwhile.

Chapter 1
Historical Background
of the Present Penal System

At the beginning of the 19th Century there were five types of prisons in Ireland: County Jails, Debtors' Prisons, Bridewells, Manor Prisons and Felon Prisons. The County Jails, in operation since about 1640, and the Bridewells, small prisons attached to police barracks, established in 1553, which held the majority of the prison population, were mostly used as holding depots before conviction. On conviction a prisoner was executed, mutilated or transported. Short-term prisoners were held in the County Jails, but transportation to the colonies was the principal solution to dealing with crime until the American War of Independence in 1776 brought this outlet to an end. The result was appalling overcrowding in prisons. Reform of the system was encouraged by people like John Howard[1] but when Australia was opened up in the 1780s as a place to transport criminals, it took the urgency out of the appeals for reform. Prisoners could be kept in irons and in dungeons; there was no separation of male and female prisoners, nor of the sane from the insane; prisoners paid for their own upkeep; prison labour became compulsory and was provided for by the notorious treadmills.

19th Century Reforms

In 1826 a major governmental enquiry into Irish Prisons took place and resulted in the Prisons Act of 1826[2]. This was the first major prisons Act in Ireland. It repealed all previous enactments relating to 'Gaols, Bridewells, Workhouses, Houses of Correction or other Prisons' and laid down rules in relation to the organisation and management of prisons and the classification of prisoners. It also made provision for a major building programme for prisons. A Board of Superintendents to administer all prisons was instituted.

The onset of the Tithe War in 1830[3] sparked off a major explosion of rural agrarian crime in Ireland, opposition to tithes leading to violent clashes between the forces of law and the peasantry. Compared to the trend in other countries where crime tended to increase with the urbanisation of the population, in Ireland the shift was from urban to rural crime because of the harsh effects of the oppressive social system on the peasantry. The Government adopted a tough line on law and order, but by the 1840s crime had reached epidemic proportions in Ireland, and the acute economic distress caused by the Famine from the mid-forties only made matters worse. Then in 1847 the passage to Van Dieman's Land (present-day Tasmania) closed down, and the resultant over-crowding, coupled with the effects of the Famine, led to disease and death for large numbers of prisoners.

Reforms of Sir Walter Crofton, 1854

To house the large prison population, more prisons were built, and six were opened in the years up to 1851, including Mountjoy. The penal methods employed were, however, those suitable for institutions dealing with urban crime and took no account of the fact that the majority of prisoners were farm labourers. The closing of New South Wales to convicts in 1853 meant the substitution of penal servitude for most sentences of transportation, and it was in that context that the reforms of Sir Walter Crofton were initiated. The latter became director of Irish prisons in 1854 and began to implement his scheme for the elimination of the criminal class in Ireland. His programme for prisoners began with punishments and deprivation, then a period of intensive labour and then rehabilitation in an Intermediate Prison. The Intermediate Prisons, with their minimal security arrangements which attempted to break down the barriers between the prisoner and the community, were particularly successful and attracted the attention of penologists from all over the world. On leaving Intermediate Prison, a convict then remained under police surveillance for a period of time.

During the ten years that the Crofton system was in operation, the crime rate in Ireland dropped to one-third of what it had previously been, but the improved economic situation in the countryside and the massive emigration following the Famine were very relevant factors in the decrease.

Devon Commission of Enquiry, 1870

In England the treatment of Fenian prisoners aroused so much controversy that in 1870 a Commission of Enquiry into the Treatment of Treason-Felony Convicts in English Prisons was set up under the Earl of Devon. Its report on the treatment, diet or discipline of the convict prisons was generally favourable to the establishment, but its findings were so hedged by important qualifications as to constitute a serious indictment of the entire prison system. In 1877 the General Prisons (Ireland) Act[4] finally centralised the prison system with financial responsibility for prisons being taken over by the Government. A General Prisons Board for Ireland took over total responsibility for the administration of the prison system. The Corporation of Directors of Convict Prisons was dissolved, the offices of Inspectors General of Prisons, Director of Convict Prisons and Registrar for Criminals were abolished and their powers were transferred to the Board. The Board itself was appointed by the Lord Lieutenant and reported to him. All ordinary prisons came under the authority of the Board, and it took over 38 local County Prisons, 95 Bridewells and 4 Convict Prisons. The Board was given the task of establishing a uniform code for the management of prisons and prisoners. Visiting Committees consisting of Justices of the Peace were set up for every prison and these committees were to report on any abuses of prisoners and other matters to the Lord Lieutenant. The Act provided for the promotion of useful trades and industries among the prison population, but not with a view to rehabilitation; rather the aim was to defray the expenses of keeping prisoners. The 'penal character of prison discipline' was to be maintained, and competition with other trades and industries was to be avoided.

Royal Commission of Enquiry, 1881

A Royal Commission of Enquiry into Irish Prisons

in 1881 examined the working of the 1877 Act with a view to assimilating the Irish and English prison systems, and its recommendations were put into effect over the next 30 years. The Probation of First Offenders Act 1887, the Fine or Imprisonment Act of 1899 which provided for the substitution of imprisonment by the payment of a fine, the Criminal Justice Administration Act of 1914 which allowed time for the payment of fines, and the Prisons Act of 1907 which allowed remission of sentence for good behaviour all helped to decrease the prison population. Until 1884 children were subjected to the same legal process as adults. In that year the Summary Jurisdiction Over Children (Ireland) Act[5] provided for the restriction on the punishment of children for summary offences to one month or less imprisonment and for the discharge of accused children and young persons without punishment for trifling offences. It also provided for the summary trial of children charged with indictable offences and the limitation of prison sentences to a period of one month. (However sentences of imprisonment could be substituted by a fine or a whipping.) It was only in 1908 that the Children Act[6] abandoned and policy of incarcerating juveniles in penal institutions and abolished the death sentence in the case of children and young persons. That Act provided instead for sending offenders and children to Reformatory and Industrial Schools, with the exception of 'unruly' or 'depraved' characters who could still be sent to prison.

Transition from Colonial to Home-Based Administration

The transition from a colonial to a home-based administration was affected from the outset by the problem of political prisoners. This would seem to have had a decisive effect on the subsequent course of penal policy in Ireland, for one of the striking features of the political situation between 1916 and 1923 was that, according as the number of political detainees went up, so the number of civilian prisoners decreased. The crime rate had not increased, but even if the law-breakers were apprehended, there was no room for them in the prisons.

At the inception of the State there were two convict prisons (Mountjoy and Portlaoise), eight local prisons, two Borstals, two Bridewells and two disused prisons at Kilmainham and Kilkenny, which had been revamped for the reception of political prisoners during the Troubles. By the time the civilian authorities took over the prisons, many were in extremely bad condition and had to be renovated or closed down — but the renovation did not extend to the penal system itself and with the ending of internment in 1924, public interest in prisons waned. The following year saw the first significant prisons' legislation of the new State, the Prisons (Visiting Committees) Act of 1925. During the debate on the proposed legislation in the Dáil[7] objection was taken to the appointment of the Committees by the Minister for Justice, and a suggestion was made that to preserve the independence of the Committees, they should be appointed by a non-governmental authority. Eventually a compromise was reached whereby no person who was in receipt of a salary paid out of the

Central Fund, other than a member of Dáil Éireann or Seanad Éireann, would be eligible for appointment to a Committee. It was clear therefore that the Committees were to be independent watchdogs of the system. Their duties were to visit the prisons frequently and to hear complaints, and to report to the Minister on any abuses observed or found by them. The Committees have, however, not tended to disagree openly with existing Departmental policy, and since they first appeared have processed only 29 complaints from prisoners. There were allegations of ill-treatment of prisoners in the years following the Act, and a Commission of Enquiry was set up in 1927 to investigate allegations made by prisoners in County Waterford. However, the Commission's report was not made public. Then in 1928 the General Prisons Board (Transfer of Functions) Order transferred the jurisdiction and functions of the General Prisons Board to the Minister for Justice and gave sole responsibility for all prisons to the Minister. By that year the prison population had declined to 728 from 3,910 in 1878.[8]

Prison Conditions Report, 1946

In 1946 concern for the treatment of prisoners forced the Minister for Justice to permit a four man committee from the Labour Party to visit Portlaoise. The Committee published a pamphlet containing their report on the visit entitled 'Prisons and Prisoners in Ireland'[9] in which they criticised the existing system. '. . . . . There remains to be considered whether our prison system, as such, is the best that can be devised for combatting crime. We are convinced that it is not the best system, that it in fact is demoralised and outmoded.... Nothing is done, or, under the present system, can be done, to improve morally or intellectually, the person sent to penal servitude..... The present system of imprisonment, so far as penal servitude prisoners are concerned, must be abandoned. In our view, the time has therefore arrived when the grey ugliness of massive stone walls should disappear and persons sentenced to terms of penal servitude sent to a place of rescue rather than to dehumanising punishment.'

The year after the publication of that Report the Prison Rules of 1826 and 1877 were updated and replaced by the Government of Prison Rules 1947. However, it was not until 1960 that a serious change in legislation of prisons took place with the passing of the Criminal Justice Act 1960. That Act enabled the granting of temporary release to prisoners and also allowed for the committal of male convicts aged between 16 and 21 directly to St. Patrick's Institution rather than having to be transferred there from adult prisons. Prison conditions had improved by then in terms of facilities and privileges, the non-use of corporal punishment, and the remission of sentences for good behaviour. However, educational, training and psychiatric and welfare services still did not exist. The prison population in 1960 was a daily average of 400, with a high percentage of short-term sentence prisoners (60% serving sentences of under 3 months).[10]

Inter-Departmental Committee, 1964

There was still much pressure on the Department of Justice to improve prison conditions and in 1962 an Inter-Departmental Committee on the Prevention of Crime and Treatment of Offenders was set up by the Government under the Chairmanship of the Secretary of the Department of Justice. Its purpose was to enquire into the prevention of crime and treatment of offenders (Dáil Reports 6th February 1964). However, its reports or recommendations were never published. It does appear from what the Minister for Justice (Mr. Haughey) said in the Dáil that the recommendations had as their aim 'the social rehabilitation of the offender' and that the recommendations were accepted. The 1960s would then mark a change in commitment to rehabilitation as being one of the purposes of imprisonment. The Prison Study Group[11] identified the main questions examined and proposals made by the Inter-Departmental Committee, and what was done about them. In the area of training, a Corrective Training Centre was set up in one of the wings of Mountjoy Male Prison with a programme of 'corrective training' almost exclusively reserved for 'first-timers'. But, as the Study Group points out, 'since there was no special system of education or training provided, there was no means of assessing the prisoners on any other basis than their conformity to discipline'. The system was considered by the authorities to be a rehabilitation programme, but in reality the Corrective Training was a system of rewards for good conduct. In regard to welfare, two welfare officers were appointed in 1964 to assist prisoners in looking for work or accommodation, but the service was quite inadequate.[12] As for Education, the Committee recommended the establishment of a school in the Corrective Training Wing. However, from the survey of offenders at St. Patrick's carried out by the Department of Psychology at U.C.D.,[13] and the

Visiting Committee to St. Patrick's Report for 1967,[14] it appears that the facilities for education and training fell far short of being an adequate system.

CHAPTER 1

1. 1726-1790
2. An act for consolidating and amending the laws relating to Prisons in Ireland, 7 Geo. IV 1826 Cap. 74.
3. The war was peasantry opposition to the payment of tithes, taxes on the produce of land for the benefit of the Anglican Church.
4. 40 and 41 Vict. 1877 Cap. 49.
5. 47 and 48 Vict. Ch. 19.
6. 8 Edw. 7 Ch. 67.
7. Dáil Reports 1925 Vol. 10.
8. The Prison Study Group: An Examination of the Irish Penal System Nov. 1973.
9. A Report on Certain Aspects of Prison Conditions in Portlaoise Convict Prison 1946.
10. Dáil Reports 1960 Vol. 183.
11. An Examination of the Irish Penal System. Nov. 1973.
12. Dáil Reports, Estimates for Vote of the new office of Minister for Justice 1969.
13. A Survey of Boys in St. Patrick's Institution. Project on Juvenile Delinquency. *The Irish Jurist* 1967.
14. Department of Justice: Annual Report on Prisons for the Year 1967.

Chapter 2
The Irish Penal System Today

There are at the present time in Ireland ten prisons and places of detention, nine of which are administered by the Department of Justice. They are:

1. *Mountjoy* — a committal prison for male and female prisoners

2. *Limerick* — a committal prison for male and female prisoners

3. *Cork* — a prison for male prisoners only

4. *Arbour Hill* — a prison for male prisoners only

5. *Portlaoise* — a prison for male prisoners, and housing mostly those convicted of or in custody charged with political offences

6. *Training Unit* — a rehabilitation centre where male adult prisoners may receive industrial training at Glengarriff Parade, Dublin

7. *Shelton Abbey* — an 'open' rehabilitation centre for male adult prisoners at Arklow, Co. Wicklow

8. *St. Patrick's Institution* — a detention centre for male juveniles between the ages of 17 and 21 at North Circular Road, Dublin 7

9. *Shanganagh Castle* — an 'open' detention centre for male juveniles at Shankill, Co. Dublin

10. *Curragh Detention Unit** — a detention centre administered by the Dept. of Defence

The prison population in May 1980 was 1,200 prisoners in custody, with another 1,600 offenders on probation. This is a 200% increase on the prison population since 1960.

Those convicted of serious crimes of a political nature are held in Portlaoise. In the Curragh prisoners who are described by the Minister for Justice as 'known trouble-makers and known disrupters' and who 'cannot be held in safety elsewhere' are held.[1]

Irish Penal Policy

There is still no discernible overall policy regarding the purpose of imprisonment. The 1877 General Prisons (Ireland) Act indicated in section 13 that punishment was the only purpose of imprisonment when it sought to secure by rules the observance of a difference between the treatment of persons unconvicted of crime, and in law presumably innocent, during the period of their detention in prison for safe custody only, and the treatment of (convicted) prisoners. . . in prison for the purpose of punishment.

The Prevention of Crime Act 1908 had the declared aim of preventing crime and 'for that purpose to provide for the reformation of 'Young Offenders' ', but for habitual offenders it provided, not for reformation, but for 'prolonged detention'. The Criminal

---

* Normally the Curragh has been used for the detention of Military offenders, but it has been used since 1972 as a prison for a small number of civilian prisoners. These prisoners, numbering about 27 are held in custody by military personnel in accordance with the Military Custody Regulations of 1972.

33

Justice Administration Act of 1914 aimed at reducing the number of cases committed to prison by facilitating the payment of fines, but in relation to young offenders and their 'treatment and punishment' it only extended the probation system, and otherwise opted out of caring for young offenders by subsidising societies that would offer to do the caring instead.

The 1960s did see a change in penal policy when, according to the then Minister for Justice in 1962, the recommendations of the Inter-Departmental Committee had 'in the main, as their aim, the social rehabilitation of the offender'.[2] Then, in the Prison Act of 1970, rehabilitation of offenders was specifically expressed to be the purpose of that legislation when it enabled provision to be made for the detention of convicted persons in places 'other than prisons'. But that Act did not contain an overall policy. Rehabilitation was limited to certain classes of person to be specified by the Minister for Justice. It was under that Act that the Training Unit at Glengarriff Parade, Shelton Abbey and Shanganagh Castle were established.

Prison Rules

The rules in force for the government of prisons are still those of 1947. The Rules deal with 'Accommodation, General Treatment of Prisoners, Employment within Prison', etc. They are generally restrictive, requiring a strict adherence to prison discipline, with sanctions for failure to do so. There is provision for 'productive labour' such as may fit the prisoner to earn his livelihood on release, and for improvement through the provision of instruction in reading, writing and arithmetic, and a library. However, it was repeatedly suggested in evidence to the Commission that these facilities were hopelessly inadequate and in no way capable of equipping prisoners for employment or betterment on their release. Indeed the Visiting Committee to St. Patrick's Institution stated in their Report for 1973 that 'the greatest obstacle to successful rehabilitation is the failure of an inmate to secure early employment'. By the time the 1979 Report of the Visiting Committee to the Institution was published the introduction of an Intensive Supervision Scheme appeared to have had some influence for the better and there were also improvements in the educational facilities which, it was felt by the Committee, greatly assisted in rehabilitation.[3]

The Rules provide that prisoners awaiting trial are treated more leniently than, and kept separate from, convicted prisoners. Juvenile offenders also receive special treatment by the mitigation of ordinary prison discipline, and such a prisoner is to be instructed as far as possible 'in a trade which may be useful to him on release'. However, it was suggested in evidence to the Commission that recidivism among juvenile offenders is high (as much as 60%) and that this is partly on account of the educational instruction being inadequate. The evidence on the rate of recidivism is confirmed by the Annual Report on Prisons for 1979[4] which states that of the 2,025 persons committed on conviction that year, 50% had previously served a prison sentence.

Education and Training Facilities

From the evidence received and from its examination of published reports of the Department of Justice, it appears to the Commission that 'reformation' of prisoners is principally associated with religious instruction and that rehabilitation programmes are not only limited to a small number of prisoners, but are inadequate even for these. The emphasis in the majority of institutions is still on security and containment, not on rehabilitation.

Educational facilities are now available in all institutions, but the whole-time teacher allocation in 1979 was only 48 among a daily average number of prisoners of 1,140. There is a serious problem in that the educational programmes are dependent on staff from outside educational units which, until 1980, did not function for three months of the year. Consequently some short-term prisoners would not benefit at all, and others had a serious disruption in their studies. The summer disruption has now been solved by the availability of teachers over the summer months, according to the Minister for Justice (speaking in May 1980)[5] although this may not occur in fact until 1981, according to the Visiting Committee to St. Patrick's Institution Report for 1979. Another problem of part-time educational staff is that the education of an individual cannot be concentrated on his particular needs and abilities. Work training facilities are presently available only at Arbour Hill and Glengarriff Parade,* although intended for all institutions. These facilities consist of an AnCO approved course in welding, machine operation,

---

* The Commission commends the excellent facilities at Glengarriff Parade, but regrets: (i) that they are available to so few prisoners, and (ii) that similar standards have not been achieved throughout the prison system.

general engineering, etc. Other prisoners are employed in baking, catering, printing, etc.

Prisoners are often engaged in work to benefit the handicapped and deprived, but without actually becoming involved with the people towards whom their work is directed. Only three institutions in 1979 were involved in projects among the community. These projects have been so successful, however, that it is hoped to extend them to the other institutions.[6]

The Commission heard evidence to the effect that in the Curragh Detention Unit there is very little occupation or training for prisoners and that what work is available is neither useful nor purposeful.

Cost of the Irish Prison System

To those who may argue that the cost of penal reform, including prevention and rehabilitation into society, is prohibitive, it must be pointed out that the existing cost of our penal system is extremely high and that it has not provided an effective remedy. The following table, which is taken from official sources, i.e. Appropriation Accounts (1971-79), shows the alarming rise in annual expenditure since 1970.

A new prison is being built in Portlaoise which it is estimated will cost more than £10,000,000 by completion. It is costing £600,000 this year (1980) and an expenditure of £4,000,000 will be incurred in 1981.

The above costs (Table No. 1) do not include expenditure on the Curragh prison or on Loughan House.

The Commission notes with dismay the low level

of spending on Welfare and Education in the Prisons.*

Table 1: Expenditure on Irish Prisons 1970-79

Year	Amount Spent	Actual Av. Daily No. of Prisoners
To 31st March '71:	£ 602,028	804
To 31st March '72:	£1,135,090	956
To 31st March '73:	£2,054,246	1,010
To 31st March '74:	£3,304,087	954
(9 months) April-Dec '74:	£3,437,534	961
To 31 Dec '75:	£5,841,813	997
To 31 Dec '76:	£6,164,325	1,047
To 31 Dec 78:	£9,489,948	1,179
To 31 Dec 79:	£13,125,906	1,140

The following figures for 1978 will illustrate this (from the Appropriation Accounts):

NET TOTAL EXPENDITURE:	£9,489,948
WELFARE SERVICES:	118,558
EDUCATIONAL SERVICES:	35,819

* On publication of the PRO Report, the Minister for Justice (Mr Gerard Collins, T.D.) pointed out that, in addition, 48 full time teachers are paid out of the Department of Education vote.

Given the undisputed fact that the majority of prisoners come from the most educationally deprived sector of society, the low level of spending on education and welfare is a sad reflection on the efforts being made to help them.

For example, more than twice the Education amount is spent on 'Post Office Services' (78,342). More than twice the Welfare Expenditure goes on 'Travelling and Incidental Expenses" (252,095).

It will be evident from our recommendations that we wish for a much larger expenditure on welfare services generally. As a further comment, we recommend that education of prisoners be given an absolute priority over any other activity inside the prisons. It is the *smallest item* of expenditure on the 1978 Appropriations for Prison Spending.

Health Care and Social Welfare of Prisoners

Medical, psychological and psychiatric services are now available in all institutions, but the Commission heard submissions to the effect that they are inadequate and that, in some cases, drugs are used with the intention of keeping prisoners quiet and docile rather than giving them curative therapy or treatment. The Inter-Departmental Committee on Mentally Ill and Maladjusted Persons has drafted legislation to provide for the detention of persons in need of psychiatric assessment or treatment in designated centres where they would be treated as patients rather than prisoners, and the Draft Bill has just been circulated (June 1980). According to the Department's Report on Prisons for 1979, 89 prisoners were transferred in that year to mental hospitals, mostly on account of schizophrenia or depression.

Parole or 'temporary release' as it is operated in Ireland is most often a daily temporary release which allows the offender to leave prison each morning and return there each night. Full temporary release is only given to enable an offender to take up employment and for the period concerned he lives at home or in a flat or hostel under the supervision of a Welfare Officer. In 1979, 342 prisoners were allowed a period of daily temporary release, and 773 were allowed full temporary release. With week-end leave and Christmas leave, the total number of daily releases was 2,842. However, it is not clear from the statistics whether certain prisoners benefitted from successive periods of release and what number of prisoners were involved in the total number of releases. But even given the apparently high number of releases, it was submitted to the Commission that it was not as high as it could be. It was submitted by professional social workers that much more week-end release would not present as great a security risk as is feared by the authorities. It appears that the break-down rate whereby offenders breached the conditions of their release is estimated by the Department at only 5%.

As previously stated, a Welfare Service was introduced into the prisons in 1964. This service was revised in 1971. It covers both prisoners and those offenders who are put on probation by the courts. The Commission heard evidence from several sources of two major problems which render the service inadequate. One is the lack of professional training among many of the social workers. Only 14% have professional training and only 40% have any training at all. The second problem is the large number of offenders which a welfare officer may have to supervise at any one time. It is not unusual for an officer to have responsibility for 17 or 18 offenders at a time. An Intensive Supervision Scheme came into operation in 1979 for the 16-21 age group, and here it is the stated intention of the Department to have only five or six offenders under the care of a welfare officer. In 1980, 13 months after the scheme had started, according to the Minister for Justice, there were nine welfare officers and three senior officers assigned to the scheme, and the number of offenders under supervision was 50. This is a very small number to benefit by the scheme, and while the Minister hoped that the number would increase to 150 by the end of 1980, the Commission heard a submission to the effect that there was a serious lack of planning in the operation of the scheme.

From the evidence that it received, from the joint and individual experience of its members and from the legislation and Departmental Reports it studied, the Commission has come to the conclusion that imprisonment in Irish society is seen as a method of protecting society and of punishing offenders. Some effort and commitment has certainly been made towards the rehabilitation of offenders in the last twenty years. Nevertheless there remains a strong element of retribution in sentencing and in the subsequent treatment of prisoners. There is very little scope for judges to exercise discretion in dealing with offenders, in any event.

The Commission was presented with several submissions relating to the care of offenders which led it to conclude that to a large degree the imprisonment of an offender was seen as an end in itself. The Minister for Justice described himself in the debate in

Seanad Éireann in May 1980 as having as his objective the providing of decent humane conditions for prisoners and 'with assistance first to make their imprisonment as tolerable as possible and, second, to help them to make the best use of their time so that they will be well equipped for their return to society'. The Commission, however, has found no evidence of an adequate commitment to rehabilitation, no concrete suggestions in relation to alternatives to custody, no suggestions at all in relation to decriminalisation which would reduce the prison population, and no apparent awareness of the link between crime and urban poverty from the Government or the Department of Justice.

The Commission accepts the incontrovertible link between social and economic deprivation and the crimes for which most people are actually imprisoned. Until the general public is convinced of this, it cannot be expected to endorse a practical attitude to decriminalisation and reduction of the prison population as well as adequate rehabilitation programmes.

The Curragh Camp Detention Unit

The prison at the Curragh Military Camp provides probably the most bizarre aspect of our entire prison system. According to the Minister for Justice, there were (in May 1980) 28 prisoners detained there. Three of them were detained in the Curragh because they required 'a high degree of security which cannot be provided elsewhere in the civil prisons'. The other 25 were there because according to the Minister they were 'known trouble-makers, and disruptive'. From the evidence tendered to us, it appears that a number of the prisoners detained there were considered to require psychiatric treatment, and were, in fact, being given medication for some form of psychiatric complaint. If the prisoners in the Curragh require psychiatric treatment, they should not be there. They should be in a psychiatric hospital.

Successive Visiting Committees appointed by the Government have commented adversely on the Curragh Military Unit. In its Report presented in early 1977, the Visiting Committee stated:

> The Committee wishes again to draw attention to the previous Report in which it stated that the Military Detention Barracks is not at all suitable for prisoners serving long sentences. The type of prisoners admitted to the prison raises difficulties regarding the provision and maintenance of gainful labour and employment. The employment available is not sufficient, and of a kind most unsuitable for preparing prisoners to earn their livelihood on release, nor are these facilities suitable for prisoners serving long sentences. This insufficiency is met to a degree by the revision of the Art and English classes. However, there is a requirement for Workshops or some facilities. There is a lack of facilities for the rehabilitative training of prisoners in Military custody. The Committee is aware that in a prison with a population of between 22 and 27 prisoners, the provision of such facilities might be disproportionately costly, and not get full usage.

In the same Report, under the title of 'Psychiatric Treatment', the Visiting Committee stated:

During the past year the Committee made recommendations concerning the availability of psychiatric facilities. Prisoners who had been receiving treatment for psychiatric disorders prior to their transfer to Military custody, continued to require treatment subsequent to their transfer. Due to the fact that there are no psychiatric facilities in the prison, treatment is limited to medication. This situation is unsatisfactory. The Committee strongly recommends that prisoners requiring psychiatric treatment should not be transferred to Military custody in the future.

Similar criticism was voiced in subsequent reports of the Visiting Committees.

The Commission of Enquiry into the Irish Penal System has no hesitation in recommending that the continued detention of civilian prisoners in the Curragh Military Detention Centre should be discontinued at the first possible opportunity.

CHAPTER 2

1. Seanad Debates. 14th May 1980. Vol. 94.
2. Dept. of Justice: Annual Report on Prisons 1978.
3. Dept. of Justice: Annual Report on Prisons 1979.
4. Ibid.
5. Seanad Debates. 14th May 1980. Vol. 94.
6. Dept. of Justice: Annual Report on Prisons 1979.

Chapter 3
The Prison Population

In this chapter we attempt to establish as broad a perspective on the prison population as our information allows, to personalise the inmates so that they take shape as individuals with distinctive social backgrounds that go far beyond the commission of whatever offence they happen to be in prison for. It is not an easy task, for the official statistics tell us little more than the numbers in prison, their respective ages and sex, the length of their sentences and whether or not they have been in prison before. It is a limited and crude picture, which sees the criminal solely in terms of his offence, his past prison experience, his age and sex, without reference to the full social and personal context within which he exists. It is a sad indictment of our criminal justice system that no official attempt has been made to understand fully the nature of crime in this country or to assess the efficacy of our response to it. If we have information which helps us towards such an understanding then it is little thanks to findings made available to us from official sources, but more to voluntary organisations or dedicated individuals, working usually against a backdrop of non-cooperation from Government departments and with poor financial resources. Such factors render our information incomplete and some might say suspect, but it is encouraging to note that, despite the inherent limitations, such information as we have available matches closely the results of much more extensive and sophisticated research in Great Britain, Europe and America, and leads inevitably to the conclusion that the vast bulk of the kind of activity which we identify as crime here in Ireland is inextricably linked to poverty and disadvantage, political, social, economic and educational.

What the Official Story Tells Us

The Annual Report of the Garda Síochána for 1978[1] recorded the commission of almost 62,000[2] indictable crimes, over half of them committed in the Dublin Metropolitan area. The category of offences referred to as indictable spans a huge array of crimes against the person and against property ranging from murder to simple larceny, but it excludes virtually all 'traffic or driving' offences except dangerous driving causing serious injury or death. However, only a very tiny minority (5%) of the recorded indictable crimes did in fact involve violence to the person. 95% were directed solely and specifically against property. In 1978 the total value of the property involved was £10,000,000, ie. an average of under £170 per crime. What is more, the vast majority of offenders were engaged in petty, unsophisticated crime — 33% were involved in burglaries, 23% in larcenies from unattended vehicles and 40% in other non-violent crimes against property. Only 4% were involved in crimes against property in which violence was used. It is a pattern which changes only marginally from year to year, and it indicates a preoccupation on the part of our entire criminal justice system with the small-time offender engaged in relatively trivial offences.

What the Official Statistics Cannot Tell Us

Why we should invest huge resources in terms of both time and money in the pursuit of the petty offender is problematic, and raises profound political and sociological questions. While realising that we are ill-equipped to answer those questions it is nonetheless pertinent that they should be mooted. Until we understand why certain types of deviance are singled out from the rest for the special scrutiny of the criminal justice system, we will never fully understand the nature of criminality in this country. Even a cursory look at our present system reveals remarkable inconsistencies. Why, for example, are we happy to allow some disputes to be resolved through the civil law while imposing criminal sanctions on others not too dissimilar e.g., the trader who deals in shoddy or substandard goods, the shop-keeper who overcharges? Why do we criminalise the man who steals a few pence worth of groceries and at the same time show a marked reluctance to use criminal sanctions against the tax evader? Would it not be appropriate for the Criminal Law spotlight to turn on the activities of home and foreign based firms who may indulge in seriously anti-social procedures and sharp practices? Why do many firms turn a blind eye to employees' thefts of goods and equipment, euphemistically terming it 'office or stock' shrinkage? Is our criminal justice system locked into 19th century notions about crime, straitjacketed by outdated and antiquated legislation which simply cannot respond to the fast changing and sophisticated economic world of the late twentieth century? Clearly there is an urgent need for reappraisal, for as it currently operates the system hooks the minnows in a narrow stretch of river, leaving the rest free for bigger and cleverer fish.

At a less theoretical and philosophical level the official statistics are again incomplete, for obviously not all those who commit crimes get caught and not all offences come to the notice of the Gardaí. Although the detection rate for crimes against the person is high (89%), for crimes against property it is a mere 36%. So at least 64 out of every 100 recorded crimes against property go undetected. Of those which are detected and result in prosecution and conviction, only one-third result in the imprisonment of the offender. Once again there is here a huge untapped area of queries about differential use of police discretion, about differential development of police resources, about the multiplicity of variable factors which go to determining which of the 36 offenders is going to be caught, arrested, charged, convicted and disposed of by imprisonment. It is an area which is likely to remain untapped, except for speculative comment based on research in other countries, until a hefty slice of official funds is thrown into investigating the significance of these matters in the operation of the penal system. Maureen Cain's study on differences between rural and urban police forces, and particularly her findings on the depths of their commitment to and communication with the community they serviced, could have parallels here, for the statistics do already show a clear divergence in degree and type of delinquency in urban and non-urban areas. Her study and others indicate a marked difference in role perspective as between urban and rural policemen. The former, seeing his function as essentially 'punitive or inquisitory' may not have the same strong local ties of the 'country cop', who by contrast sees his function as a 'peace-keeping' one. Hence the latter may develop a wide area of discretion in which local or personal resources are utilised in dealing with deviancy at a level other than official cautioning or prosecution. The 'city cop' may not have the time or opportunity to develop a strong local base; indeed he may find himself regarded as a stranger, despite his overtures. Inevitably these differing perspectives and differential role developments do create very real differences in approach to deviancy-differences which are subtle and almost imperceptible in the absence of probing investigation and analysis.

The Prison Population

In 1979, 1888[3] males and 137 females were committed to prison on conviction. 508 juveniles were sentenced to detention in St. Patrick's Institution Both adult and juvenile figures show a drop over the 1978 figures. Of these, 1971 were sentenced to terms of imprisonment and 54 to Penal Servitude. The length of sentences breaks down as follows:

Sentences of Imprisonment	Males	Females
Under 3 months	540	67
3 to 5 months	297	27
6 to 11 months	527	29
12 months	297	11
12 to 23 months	35	2
2 years	48	0
Over 2 years	109	0

Sentences of Penal Servitude		
3 to 5 yrs	26	1
6 to 10 yrs	22	0
Over 10 years	2	0

| Life .... | 3 .... | 0 |
| Sentence unknown .... | 0 .... | 0 |

The trend of offences, weighed down as it is with short terms of imprisonment imposed mainly by the District Courts, underlines again the pattern of petty offenders, committing petty offences for which they receive brief spells in prison. Serious or violent offences and lengthy periods in prison are the exception rather than the rule. If we add to this the fact that 58% of males and 41% of females sentenced in 1979 had been in prison before (25% of males and 18% of females had served 1-5 previous terms, 34% of males and 23% of females had served 5-20 previous sentences and 9-10% of both sexes had been 'inside' more than 20 times), it becomes starkly apparent that the recidivist committed to a life of petty, small-scale crime takes up the bulk of the available prison space. More than anyone he or she highlights the failure of the prison system to rehabilitate or to help in constructing an alternative and law-abiding way of life.

Female Prisoners

Though labouring for the most part under the same social disadvantages as the male prisoner, the female prisoner stands apart from the general run of criminals in more ways than one. The single salient feature is the apparent lack of criminality in women, if one were to judge by the statistics alone, for despite being 50% of the population in general women account for only a tiny proportion of the criminal population, 6.7% in 1979. With a few exceptions they were sent to prison for trifling offences such as drunkenness

(26), larceny (57), soliciting (6) and begging (2). Thirty-one were convicted of offences involving violence, such as assault or malicious damage to property. Though 137 women were sent to prison in 1978, the daily average in Mountjoy was 15, and in Limerick prison 9, which once again testifies to the brevity of the sentences imposed. An interesting aspect of the female prison population is its drastic decline over the past 50 years, from 1029 in 1929 to 137 in 1978. The Government's plan for a new female prison with accommodation for 100 is difficult to justify in the face of these statistics, and the danger is that where there is expensive space waiting to be filled then filled it will be, regardless of the suitability of custodial treatment for the offender in question. As was pointed out in a public submission on 'Women in Prison', Irish society has survived half a century during which only a tiny proportion of females have been either deviant or imprisoned. What is more, if drunkenness and soliciting were decriminalised the female prison population would be drastically reduced. What signs are there on the horizon that female criminality is likely to increase to the extent that a new institution is required? There is force indeed in the argument which says that at a time when the rest of Europe and America is acknowledging the failure of custodial treatment in its traditional form and when the search for alternatives is well on the way, what better area to experiment in than this small section of the prison population. Apart from the empirical experimental value of testing non-custodial alternatives on female offenders, the added advantage of not removing mothers from their children and homes is obvious.

The Juvenile Offender

Of the 2027 people sentenced to prison in 1978, 476 were under 21. Forty-two were females aged between 15 and 21 while 434 were males in the same age range. In addition 570 juveniles were convicted of crimes against property and again the vast majority served sentences of less than twelve months.

Social Background of Offenders

From the voluntary and professional bodies concerned in the welfare of prisoners, ex-prisoners, and their families, comes irrefutable evidence that strong causal links exist between criminality and recurring political, social, environmental and educational factors. The majority of those who end up in our prisons are born into socially disadvantaged circumstances and come from the most deprived sectors of society, in terms of income, housing, education, opportunity, mobility, environment, etc. Two surveys were carried out by the Prisoners' Rights Organisation in 1979, one of 50 children from inner city Dublin who had records for delinquency and another of 200 adult offenders. They are the only surveys of their kind and, even allowing limitations which the trained eye of the professional sociologist might detect, they are invaluable documents, providing incisive commentaries on causation in criminality. The information elicited by the surveys was substantiated again and again by the evidence of individual prisoners, by the concerned organisations which made representations to us, and by the individuals engaged in voluntary and professional care of prisoners. Over and over again, we heard of the cyclical nature of criminality and the almost invariable 'common denominators' which hallmark those whom we label prisoners.

The PRO surveys show that the majority of those interviewed were born into the grim inner city slums. They were born into large families, living in Corporation dwellings on low incomes. In many instances it was the mother, working in poorly paid cleaning jobs, who was the breadwinner and source of family income. If the father was employed it was generally in unskilled labouring and among the interviewees themselves unemployment was the norm. Few had training in skilled trades or occupations. A large number had brothers or sisters who had fallen foul of the law and about 20% admitted that one or other of their parents had a criminal record. We received evidence from other sources of poor father/son relationships, the father having a poor and demoralised self-image which resulted in the son having little to live up to by way of example (even where the parent was non-criminal). Parental failure expressed by the inability of the mother to cope with family responsibilities under extremely difficult circumstances, combined with ineffective paternal contribution and support, leads to an absence of control, guidance or discipline for the juvenile. This often culminates in delinquent conflict with the law. Although the majority of juvenile offenders disappear from the criminal statistics on reaching adulthood, for those who fail to 'reform' and who end up in prison in adulthood the pattern of criminal activity almost invariably begins in childhood.

Our low minimum age of criminal responsibility, i.e., seven, the lowest incidentally in Europe, ensures that the trivial activities of little children come under the censorious scrutiny of the criminal justice system. For many offenders, whether male or female, their criminal careers began with early experience of reformatories or industrial schools precipitated by truancy from school or home, or family break-down. Here again factors like differential police deployment can seriously affect the likelihood of a particular child becoming identified as deviant. The child in the bleak inner city, lacking private amenities like gardens or playrooms, or simply space, carries his activities onto the streets where he is in full public view. His scope for 'safe' deviancy is limited. Parents may not have money to steal or property to deface. His controls are few and he is highly visible particularly if, as there tends to be, there is a high level of police deployment in his area. There was an incredible pathos about the submission which began,

'When I was seven I was sent to Clonmel by Justice Kennedy. I was in it for nine years'.

Educational Factors

According to the PRO's adult-prisoner survey, 76% of those interviewed did not go beyond primary school; in fact, as remarked earlier, for many their first brush with the law may very well have been for truancy. One can only wonder at how far their experiences at the hands of officialdom and the legal process propelled them further into a life of crime rather than the reverse. The lack of schooling is underlined by the appalling levels of literacy and numeracy among prison inmates. At least one-third were totally illiterate on leaving school and of the rest, most had only the barest literacy competence. Nor is there any reason to believe that what they lack in academic competence they make up for in manual skills. The reverse seems to be the case, for apart from the dearth of 'job' skills, one psychologist involved in a juvenile institution claimed his research showed a consistent lack of skills involving manual and physical co-ordination.

It is scarcely surprising therefore that where educational facilities exist within the custodial system they are predominantly of a remedial nature. In the recent past new educational units have been introduced in Mountjoy and Limerick prisons and, though very limited in nature, they go some way to catering for prisoners' needs. But not far enough. Library facilities in our prisons are shamefully poverty-stricken, 'security' rules often place tight restrictions on the transferring of books between prisoners, the possession of writing materials, etc. We heard evidence from a number of people engaged in teaching in penal institutions that the attempt to graft an essentially rehabilitative function, i.e. education, onto a prison system which is fundamentally punitive in nature, has not been successful. The commitment of some of our penal institutions to education within the prison is in some doubt. Both prisoners and staff testified that education was regarded as something to be squeezed in between the more important items on the prisoners' daily agenda. For example, we were told of classes being regularly interrupted by prison security staff who would request class members to help to prepare meals or launder clothes, etc. There were allegations that some prison staff were hostile to the notion of educational facilities within prisons at all and at best they were grudgingly tolerated. These allegations did not touch on all penal institutions: some, like Shanganagh Castle, the 'open' detention centre for young offenders, clearly lay a major emphasis on education and rehabilitation, but then their whole structure, concept, facilities and staffing arrangements differ radically from the militaristic régime of the traditional penal institution, and lend themselves more easily to rehabilitative endeavours. But given the degree to which prison inmates, particularly young people, are handicapped by illiteracy, and assuming that, especially in relation to juveniles, emphasis should be on rehabilitation rather than punishment, it is scandalous that something so useful and positive as even basic education should ever take a back seat to cleaning floors and washing dishes. One striking indication of the lack of a genuine commitment to the profound need to provide educational facilities within the penal system is the consistent failure to provide any teaching facilities during the summer months. Since many juveniles find themselves detained for short spells (and since the summer often maximises their opportunity to commit crime), those who pass through the institutions during the summer months have not been receiving remedial or any teaching. An opportunity is unnecessarily wasted.

Employment

It isn't surprising, in view of the poor education attainments of prisoners generally and in view of the fact that they come often from areas of indigent, chronic unemployment, that their own employment prospects are bad also. Sixty five per cent of those in the PRO survey were seldom or never in work. As potential employees they have little to offer in terms of skills, ability or experience and of course spending time in prison does little to increase their prospects. In a country where it is difficult to get employment of the type the average prisoner could cope with, i.e.

unskilled or semi-skilled manual labour, even with an exemplary record, how much more difficult is it for those with convictions for dishonesty. In this regard the State-owned bodies have given the private sector anything but good example. Rather than taking the lead in the social re-establishment of the ex-prisoner by giving him employment they have done the reverse. There have been regrettable examples of people being sacked from 'Government' employment simply because their past record had been discovered — despite their suitability and good service in the job. The State carries its punishment of the offender unjustifiably and inhumanly far beyond the last day of imprionsment. And the inevitable Catch-22 situation arises for the ex-prisoner released onto the streets with little money, probably no accommodation, and no job prospects. Small wonder we have a high rate of recidivism!

The Annual Prison Visitors' reports do indicate steady, albeit slow progress in the development of work experience facilities within prisons, especially at Glengarriff Parade, but the position is still primitive and has a long way to advance before it makes any real inroads into the problem of equipping the prisoner for an active working life on release. The crafts and industries provided within the prisons have only a limited application to the working world and indeed more often than not are dying trades, e.g. shoemaking, tailoring, matmaking, etc. It is a problem common to all the institutions, but surely in the female prison there is no excuse for failing to provide a couple of modern light industrial machines of a relevant training nature instead of the obsolete machines they have presently, which by no stretch of the imagination could give them work-experience of use 'outside'. Clearly there are space and resource problems in providing in-training within institutions but there are other, less expensive alternatives which have been used with success on the continent. For example the employed person sent to prison could be permitted to continue his outside employment, returning to the institution at night and at weekends. Day release for prisoners to jobs or courses outside could be developed with no great danger to the public.

But some work is better than no work and the paucity of work facilities in prisons seems to hit hardest at remand prisoners. They are not obliged to work, but for many it is better than idling away the hours in manic boredom; yet where work is lacking for convicted prisoners that is precisely what the remand prisoner does. Add to that the petty restrictions on borrowing books (a very limited number per week), the fact that prisoners cannot swap books, and the already pathetic library stock. Clearly many hours are spent in prison in totally non-productive idleness which may indeed have counterproductive effects on individual prisoners, and often does. It is possible, however, to make too much of the role of prison as a rehabilitator. Many of the inmates, as we have remarked before, spend less than one year in prison at a time — and many spend much less than that. Realistically one cannot expect miracles on the education and job fronts over months where society has failed over years. This is not, however, an argument for extended sentences but rather a call for a rapid and thorough reappraisal of a system which penalises people already severely socially handicapped and for whom the cycle of prison experience and low social position virtually ensures they are trapped in lives of petty crime. Where are the sophisticated and practical after-care facilities for these people? Where are the subsidised vocational training and educational facilities, outside prison? The fact is they are virtually non-existent, and that lack again underwrites and directly contributes to persistent recidivism.

Summary

There is an indisputable pattern which attaches, with depressing monotony, the fact of criminality (as society perceives it) to deprivation and disadvantage. What is more, the connection is no accident. Why some people in some circumstances break the law has defied criminologists for decades and there is no Holy Grail, but there is a series of identified features which need to be tackled in terms of prevention for future generations. To those already caught up in the crime/ deprivation syndrome ours must seem a curious world and the words of the Constitution so many meaningless phrases. Can we claim to cherish equally the nation's children when virtually the only criminality/ deviancy/socially-disruptive behaviour we penalise is that which emanates from the most disadvantaged sections of our community? It is about time we worked out why we do this year in and year out. We need to know whether our intervention in the lives of those penalised has a function other than straightforward punishment and retribution — for clearly at that level it is a resounding success. But if we as a caring community demand more from our penal system, demand enlightenment, dignity, humanity, caring and consideration for our society's casualties, what we have is a half-baked system cemented into a 19th century developmental framework irreversibly punitive in nature, struggling to adjust to 20th century rehabilitative, reformative or simply humanitarian notions, and it is unlikely that the marriage is going to be a happy one. No-one denies the right of the state to penalise, but is it not possible to imitate some of our European neighbours and do it with compassion, understanding and above all with dignity?

CHAPTER 3

1. Last year for which figures are available.
2. A drop of 946 on 1977 Total.
3. Excluding 68 debtors and contempt of court prisoners.

Chapter 4
Alternatives to Prison and Rehabilitation of Prisoners

The treatment of prisoners while in prison and their reintegration into normal community and social life after serving their sentences have been given serious consideration by the Commission. We feel that these two questions must be central to any enquiry into our penal system. As it appears to the Commission, the present system is very inadequate in respect of both questions.

In this chapter the questions of rehabilitation through the constructive use of time spent in prison and that of the provision of an adequate post-prison reintegration programme and service are discussed. While the Commission supports a radical improvement of prison conditions and training and educational facilities, it is convinced that even after the attainment of such a radical improvement, prison of its nature militates against rehabilitation of the offender. Therefore, our strongest recommendation will be to provide alternatives to prison for as many people who are convicted by the criminal courts as is possible. The provision of suitable alternatives to prison is considered best for the offender, for society and for those who have been offended by the deviant activities of the convicted offender in most cases.

The Commission has examined and reviewed the current literature available on the success and failure of prisons as places of rehabilitation in a number of Western states with conditions not unlike those prevailing in modern Irish society and likely to develop here in the future. The following brief but relevant synopsis of views and findings from the United States, Canada, Sweden and Britain makes a *prima facie* case for new thinking on rehabilitation.

United States

Since the practice of imprisoning offenders still rests on the 19th-century concept of a prison, or penitentiary, being a place of rehabilitation (a reform first conceived by Pennsylvania Quakers in 1790) prison today is seldom *acknowledged* to be primarily a place of punishment. The Commission accordingly searched for evidence of success in rehabilitation as a justification for continuing the use of prisons on such a wide scale. They find that present-day Quakers believe that their forefathers made a serious mistake in thinking that prisons could rehabilitate. In a recent publication, *Struggle for Justice*, the American Friends Service Committee concludes that 'rehabilitation has introduced a new form of brutality, more subtle and elusive' (1971, p. 96).

The tendency to find alternatives to institutional custody has come to be generally accepted. In 1930 in the United States the Wickersham Commission made the following recommendation:

'The millions of dollars now employed to construct elaborate maximum security prisons could, with much better advantage, be used in the development and proper financing of adequate systems

62

of probation and parole'.

In 1973 the United States National Advisory Committee on Criminal Justice and Gaols in the course of its report to the President and Congress of the United States pointed out:

'The failure of major institutions to reduce crimes is incontestable. Recidivism rates are notoriously high. Institutions do succeed in punishing, but they do not deter. They protect the community but that protection is only temporary. They relieve the community by removing the offender, but they make successful reintegration into the community unlikely. They change the committed offender, but the change is more likely to be negative than positive'.

The negative effects of imprisonment on the prisoner have also been pointed out by the Advisory Committee elsewhere in the report. These include alienation, withdrawal and loss of self-confidence:

'At its worst, the prison offers an insidious false security as those who are banished return to the social scene of their former crime. The former prisoner seldom comes back the better for the experience of confinement. . . the damage that prison does is subtle. Attitudes are brutalised and self confidence is lost. The prison is a place of coercion where compliance is obtained by force. The typical response to coercion is alienation, which may take the form of active hostility to all social controls or later a passive withdrawal into alcoholism, drug addiction or dependency'.

Norman Carlson, Director of the Federal Bureau of

Prisons and President of the American Correctional Association has said (*U.S. News and World Report*, March 1st, 1976):

> 'We must phase out the penitentiary as the mainstay of our correctional system. It is too big, too costly, and too depersonalised – it is simply not effective'.

On his estimates, almost 75% of the federal population of jails could be released with no threat to the community.*

Robert Sommer in his book *The End of Imprisonment* asserts: –

> 'No-one has been able to run a decent prison – not the Quakers, not the Soviets, not the conservatives or liberals, not the counties. There is something basically wrong with the idea of forcibly removing lawbreakers from society, bringing them together in a single location, and placing them under the domination of keepers for long periods'. (1976, pp. 21-24; 182-185)

In one of his London Lectures on Contemporary Christianity, Charles Colson, author of *Born Again* and *Life Sentence*, called on Christians to think very seriously about the underlying premise of a prison.

> 'If criminal conduct is encouraged by association and environment then society needs to think very

---

* Roger Atrill, Governor of Winson Green Prison, Birmingham, in an interview published in the *New Statesman,* (19th Sept 1980) expresses a similar view and regrets that of the 4,093 prisoners who passed through his prison between 1st July 79 and 30th June 1980, 50.6%, were identified as unsuitable for imprisonment.

seriously about the rationale of punishment which puts all known criminals together in one place'.

In his work *Criminal Violence, Criminal Justice*, Charles Siberman of New York emphasises the same theme:—

> 'As instruments of punishment prisons have been a resounding success but they have never achieved their goal of rehabilitation. Over the last half-century, one crime commission after another has criticised prisons for their failure to rehabilitate inmates and has called for new approaches to achieve success. . . . The Crime Commission's faith in the possibility of rehabilitation has given way to pessimism and doubt. The last ten years have seen a flood of scholarly literature documenting the failure of one approach after another'
> (1978, p.4).

Canada

In Canada in 1976 and 1977, a special Sub-Committee on the Penitentiary System presented its *Report to Parliament*, which contained the results of long and well-documented research. The Canadian Parliamentarians had this to say:

> 'Society has spent millions of dollars over the years to create and maintain the proven failure of prisons. Incarceration has failed on its two essential purposes — correcting the offender and providing permanent protection to society. The recidivist rate of up to 80% is the evidence of both'
> (1977, p. 35)

(In Ireland, it is generally held that the rate of recidivism varies between 50% and 80%)

The Report maintains that one of the failures of the prison system involves the notion that offenders can be removed from the community and made the responsibility of 'someone else'. It emphasises the importance of community involvement in dealing with those who have broken society's laws:

'No penitentiary service can succeed without understanding and participation by the public. Prisons belong to the public and therefore the people who pay for them have a vested interest in their remaining peaceful and in serving their best interests... The community also should participate and concern itself with the job the prisons are doing, if for no other reason than for its own safety'.

Sweden

Turning to the Swedish system of correctional care, we learn from the Fact Sheet, 'Correctional Care in Sweden' (available from the Swedish Embassy):

'The foundation of Swedish correctional policy is that sanctions involving loss of liberty should be avoided wherever possible, since such sanctions do not as a rule improve the individual's chances of adjusting to a life in freedom... it is a widespread view and supported by experience that better preventive results are obtained at the individual level by correctional care outside institutions. Non-institutional care is also a more humane and a cheaper form of care than institutional. As a result of this view, significant efforts are being made to give both the public and the judicial authorities sufficient confidence in non-institutional care for it to be able to function as a fully adequate alternative to sanctions involving deprivation of liberty'.

This policy seems to comply with the recommendation of the Fifth United Nations Congress on the Prevention of Crime and the Treatment of Offenders (1975) which proposed that reliance on prison as a penal sanction should be reduced and that there should be an increase in the use of alternatives to imprisonment for those offenders who do not need to be incarcerated. It was then urged that:

'The use of imprisonment should be restricted to those offenders who needed to be neutralised in the interest of public safety, or for the protection of society'.

Britain

In Britain the all-party committee of the House of Commons has recently held an *Inquiry into the United Kingdom Prison Services*. The British National Association of Probation Officers, reporting to this Inquiry, drew attention to the fact that, in their opinion, the aims of many penal institutions are not and cannot be, in fact, as stated in the Prison Rules, etc. (viz. that 'at all times the treatment of prisoners shall be such as to encourage their self-respect and sense of personal responsibility'; 'the task of the institution is to provide, as far as possible, a régime that is humane, dignified, constructive, participatory and looks outward to the community rather than inward'.) The Association of Probation Officers finds that:—

'Experience indicates that at present the overriding priorities are those of security and control and in all too many penal institutions, the management and use of resources are geared to this above all else. We recognise the importance of security in the prison setting but there is need to establish an appropriate balance between all the needs of the inmates and the institution including training, education, employment, recreation and rehabilitation in the community'.

In the opinion of our Commission of Inquiry into the Penal System in Ireland, security and control are also overriding priorities in our penal institutions. While recognising the importance of security in the prison setting, the Commission feels that the importance of an appropriate balance cannot be too strongly stated. Where the needs of the inmates are neglected (some of whom locked together are deprived of even the most basic personal privacies), the result is detrimental not only to them but to the staff expected to operate such régimes and, in the long run, to society as a whole. The U.K. Probation Officers Association echoes the view of the American and Swedish sources already quoted when it states:—

'The rehabilitation of prisoners is normally given such a low priority at present that the net effect of a custodial sentence may well be a deterioration in an individual's ability to cope on release. We think it essential from every point of view to put more emphasis on providing alternatives to prison'.

The Association comments favourably on projects such as neighbourhood borstal schemes, now in being for five years, which have greatly strengthened the links between the institutions and the community, both in the vicinity of the borstals and in the trainees' home areas.

The Parliamentary All-Party Affairs Group (referred to above) which had a membership of over eighty, drawn from both Houses of the British Parliament and from the three major political parties, in its Report (adopted on 13th May 1980) concluded thus:

> 'Our studies have satisfied us that no lasting impression can be made upon the growing problem without a radical change in approach and attitudes. Our approach is to reserve custody, whether pre-trial or post-trial, to those who would represent a real danger to society. To those whose freedom would represent no more than a nuisance, we propose both new methods and the greater use of tried and established non-custodial methods of disposal. Radical as our proposals are, they must inevitably give a wide discretion to sentencing authorities. We believe it is vital that in the exercise of that discretion, the courts should conscientiously follow the spirit of our recommendations; that remand in custody should be wholly exceptional; that a prison sentence should be imposed only when no other is possible; that no prison sentence should be longer than is absolutely essential for the protection of society'.

Programmes of Restitution

Prisons are generally acknowledged to be successful in protecting society from their inmates for as long as the latter are contained within them. But, once released, the rate of recidivism of these offenders is, as has been said, in some jurisdictions found to be as high as 80% while nowhere could we discover a lower rate than 50%. On the other hand, current Programmes of Restitution, with or without incarceration, presently established in seven American states, are by comparison yielding remarkably low rates of recidivism (not much higher than 6%) and are costing the taxpayer less than half as much to run. Schemes of restitution, either by money or service, to the victim of a crime are open to certain types of offenders and are closely monitored by community agencies set up for the purpose. Their success is measured, not only in terms of the effect on the offender and on society in general, but also on that presently forgotten person — the victim — who, under our system of imprisonment, may be said to be twice victimised, once by the crime and later by having to contribute in taxes to the support of the perpetrator in jail. The value of a system of restitution may be considered also in terms of its beneficial effect on the community in general (where, so far in the U.S., acceptance of such schemes has been welcomed). The Judeo-Christian ethic has been one of restitution since Old Testament times, while present day sociologists and psychologists question the wisdom of hiding away offenders from the rest of the community. (Sometimes referred to as 'The Toilet Assumption',* the thinking is that readiness to forget about offensive matter once it is out of sight has led to a less human and less responsible society).

* See: Philip Slater, *Pursuit of Loneliness*, Boston 1970, p. 15.

In the Irish connection, reference may be made here to the recent remarks of Professor Patrick Hannon of Maynooth, who at the Social Study Conference in Galway, August 1980, gave a moral theologian's view of the Christian perspective of crime and punishment. Referring to recent objections by local residents in Dublin to the siting of a women's prison in their midst, Dr. Hannon found this:

> '. . . .difficult to reconcile with a sense of community responsibility and even more difficult to reconcile with the profession of Christian belief. . .'

In somewhat the same vein, Father Kevin Mullen writing in *The Furrow*, August 1980, treats of the Christian perspective on the death penalty and calls for a greater sense of responsibility from the community, saying:

> '. . . . it will never be possible to banish all risk from the human community. In the long run, our own selfishness, venality, covetousness, unconcern and irresponsibility which generate victims amongst us and spawn criminals, constitute the greater risk for all of us'.

Attention was drawn by Professor Hannon to the unsatisfactory nature of our prison Visiting Committees and he called for much greater freedom of access to prisons which should be open to any person 'with legitimate interest'. (It is relevant to mention here that few members of our Commission, which includes elected representatives, university teachers, an internationally acclaimed authority on human rights, a prominent Trade Unionist, and a sociologist, could gain access to any of our jails before producing this Report).

In an impressive study entitled *Restitution as an Alternative Prison,** Professor Daniel H. Benson (Associate Professor of Law at Texas University) and Charles W. Colson (Founder of Prison Fellowship, Washington D.C.) give convincing evidence of the comparative success of pilot schemes of restitution now established in seven American states, concluding:

> 'We insist that whether a properly designed and operated restitution programme will work is no longer open to question; experience establishes that such programmes can and do work. Whatever the theoretical arguments in opposition to such programmes may be. . . the fact is that such programmes can and do work well'.

In this context the Commission welcomes the remarks of Mr. Collins, Minister for Justice, in a Seanad Éireann debate on 14th May 1980, in relation to *Community Service Orders:*

> 'The Department of Justice are examining the possibility of introducing legislation to empower the courts to impose community service orders as an alternative to custody. This proposal requires extremely careful and detailed analysis and it will take some time to formulate a final scheme'.

> (para. 333, Official Report of Seanad Éireann 1980)

The Commission recommends that the efforts of the Department of Justice to prepare legislation for the introduction of Community Service Orders as an

* The basis of a London Lecture on 'Contemporary Christianity', Spring 1979.

alternative to custodial sentences should be a matter of priority.

REHABILITATION OR RECIDIVISM?

The Commission agrees with the view that prison is probably the least suitable environment for the proper reintegration of the offender into society. It nevertheless is aware of the unlikelihood of the decline of the use of prisons in the near future. We therefore urge a radical change of the prison routine to enable those confined to utilise their time in prison for educational training and occupational programmes which will contribute to the prisoner's rehabilitation. By rehabilitation is meant the reintegration of the offender into his or her community and society.

Main Conditions of Rehabilitation

The reintegration of the prisoner into society is best guaranteed by the following conditions:

(a) The guarantee of continuous *social and personal contact* with family and friends as far as possible to reduce the social insulation of the prisoner while in prison. Where possible parole for the purpose of visitation to family and friends should be granted regularly.

(b) The provision of *living conditions* conducive to the maintenance of self-respect and human dignity. Unnecessarily demeaning conditions are likely to lead to serious demoralisation. The provision of worthy human conditions includes: proper living quarters; proper recreational and cultural facilities; adequate facilities for sport and physical education; adequate medical and counselling services; proper spiritual and religious services, and a Warden's code of behaviour with prisoners which respects the human dignity of the prisoner. Mutual respect between prisoners should also be encouraged.

(c) The third condition is that of adequate *education, training and occupation* of the prisoner which will improve his or her chances of returning to socially useful and personally satisfying employment on completion of sentence. Because of the deprived socio-economic background of many offenders, and the diversity of standards and their occupational orientations, a proportionately large educational and training staff will be required to give adequate attention to the needs of each individual prisoner. Much remedial education will also be required. In general, however, there should be a distinction between the needs of younger and of more mature offenders. Special programmes should be designed to suit both categories.

(d) The involvement and cooperation of *extra-prison agencies* is imperative to the success of any programme of rehabilitation. The agencies include:
Educational Agencies, i.e. voluntary and statutory bodies (including AnCO);
Trade Unions, who can facilitate the reintegration of ex-prisoners into the work-force;
Employers, whose willingness to employ ex-prisoners is an essential condition for the successful reintegration (Employers include

State and Semi-State Bodies);
Social Welfare Agencies, who will provide the
necessary financial and social support for the
person on completion of a prison sentence
especially during the vital transition period
immediately after release.

Prevention of Recidivism

In this paragraph the Commission addresses itself
to the concrete problem arising from the present
prison position in Ireland. From the submissions
made to the Commission, it would appear that
the penal system is not succeeding in its task of
preventing recidivism. Perhaps the most important
element in breaking the cycle of recidivism is rehabilitation, particularly after an initial committal
or non-committal sentence on young persons.

While everyone would agree with this valuable
aspiration, the practical arrangements, including
institutions, staff and funding, are another matter.
Many would argue that social and environmental
deficiencies in the first instance largely create the
objective conditions that lead to criminal offences
and society at large is indifferent to cause and effect.
Therefore rehabilitation in these circumstances, it is
argued, is irrelevant as a serious measure in breaking
the recidivist cycle.

In support of this latter argument in his submission to the Commission, the Rev. Brian Power
says:

'At least in the majority of cases which I have
encountered of boys who were in continual conflict
with the law, family or local environment was in
some way oppressive or inadequate. Research in

general indicates that this is invariably so. Consequently preventive measures* which would improve the quality of family and community life should receive the greatest support and funding in any drive to solve delinquency problems'.

Nevertheless, in this exercise the Commission cannot dodge the issue of rehabilitation because of imperfections in our economic and social order (which are generally regarded as not conducive to the establishment of good citizenship, based on social justice and human dignity).

The Prisoners' Rights Organisation, in their analysis of age and social origins of first offenders from a survey of ex-prisoners carried out for them state that 51% were first convicted between 11 and 15 years and 24% were first convicted between 16 and 21 years. This then throws the emphasis on the way society deals with the young delinquent, and raises the question of the urgent need for immediate improvement in the areas of counselling, group therapy, education and training, family involvement before and after release, and the raising of the level of professionalism in the custodial system at all levels.

School/Family Counselling Service

Again, the work done by the PRO on the question of what they term 'functional literacy' would show that the vast majority of offenders had a very low level of literacy. One-third indeed could not read

---

* As instances of appropriate preventive measures the Commission notes with approval the work of Extern in Belfast and the recent project announced by Aston Villa Football Club in England to provide training for youthful fans.

or write when leaving school and the supportive role of the family was almost non-existent; the families were large and the parents also lacked steady employment or formal educational achievement.

This being so, latent delinquency identified at primary school level by recurring absences, late coming, indolence and violent attitudes, should be notified by the teacher to a *School/Family Counselling Service* run and financed by the Local Authority. The School/Family Counsellor would then assess the family circumstances and the community influences at work and seek to secure family support for the child.

This may also involve, where children have been before the Courts, liaison with community welfare officers, probation officers, teachers, and, at secondary school level, the Industrial Training Authority and Manpower Services.

For the most mature and married offenders, education and training of a socially useful nature during detention is an absolute must. The unskilled nature of prison work is punitive rather than rehabilitative. Who makes mailbags outside prison in a commercial way?

It should be the responsibility of the State to insist that offenders who, during detention, showed aptitudes and skills in Education and Training Programmes be placed either in employment in the private and public sector or facilitated to continue their education and training on maintenance grants equal to average industrial earnings. The Ministers for Labour and Justice should underpin this approach by legislation. On the question of the employment of offenders post-detention the public sector, central and local, would seem to have a very poor record.

Indeed, there are many instances recorded of the management of public bodies sacking an employee on spurious grounds where an earlier prison sentence was not revealed on appointment. Unfair dismissals legislation will be some protection against such victimisation in the future.

Council for the Rehabilitation of Offenders

In the whole process of rehabilitative work and education in and out of detention, the Trade Unions and Employer Organisations should be involved also in a *Council for the Rehabilitation of Offenders* through their local organisations. In addition, both sides of industry, through their organisations, should have a continuing presence on *Visiting Committees* to allow assessment at first hand of the situation.

All of this, of course, requires that the Department of Justice, Education, and Labour, and the Local Authorities have the necessary will to establish the structures and provide the funds for a new comprehensive programme for prophylatic and rehabilitative procedures to prevent crime and social misdemeanours and to try and deal with recidivism which, in human and social and economic terms, costs society much more to ignore than to deal with.

Violence against the person, petty crime and vandalism will not be corrected by building larger punitive institutions. Some people would have us believe that the deterrent effect of being held in custody is the answer. The Minister for Justice and other interested persons know that detention, as it is now administered, will not deter but can and does, by its stigmatism, social ostracism and the absence of post-detention rehabilitation and support, create the objective circumstances of the *offence-detention-offence cycle*. Some offenders describe detention as an 'occupational hazard' and to those offenders who live on the streets it is looked on as an improvement in the material circumstances of their existence for as long as they stay in custody. The State must pay something like £180 or more per week in total for their care in custody, nine times more than an old age pensioner gets to keep body and soul together.

Conclusion

In the section devoted to the question of rehabilitation, i.e. the reintegration of the offender into society on completion of his or her sentence, the main conditions likely to make rehabilitation possible have been given. These include social and personal contact between prisoner and family and friends during sentence, decent living conditions in prison, the provision of adequate education, training and occupation of prisoners, and the effective involvement and cooperation of extra-prison agencies relevant to successful rehabilitation.

The problem of rehabilitation of prisoners in Irish prisons today and in the near future has also been discussed. The alternative to the absence of a more effective policy and programme of rehabilitation is the undesirable, but inevitable, continuity or even increase of the rate of recidivism. The Commission is of the opinion that the present situation is detrimental to both the prisoner and society and calls for a radical reappraisal of the system.

Chapter 5
Conclusions and Recommendations

Since the foundation of the State there has been no reappraisal of the purpose and function of prisons by those in authority. Our Commission, in default of a Government enquiry, has considered the need to examine the effectiveness of this inherited system. We find that the cost to the tax-payer of containment of prisoners in our jails — over £9,000 per prisoner per annum — is not met by a similarly high rate of success in correcting offenders. Recidivism running at 60% does not in our view justify this expenditure.

Members of the Commission have studied models of *alternatives to prison* suited as punishment for non-violent offenders. They have been looking at experiments in Britain and in Northern Ireland as well as at Swedish and American models.

The overall aim of the law enforcement policies of the State should be:

(a) To remove wherever possible the circumstances that lead to the commission of certain types of offences. For instance, to provide in urban areas wherein housing conditions are unsatisfactory, small schools, social centres and other amenities that will provide occupation and activities for juveniles.

(b) To use imprisonment only as a last resort, and in cases where the safety of society requires it. Suitable alternatives to imprisonment should be considered in each case with great care.

(c) The aim of any sentence, custodial or otherwise, should be the eventual integration of the offender into society. In particular, very special efforts should be made to ensure that each offender, upon the termination of his or her sentence, should be able to obtain employment and reasonably good housing conditions.

(d) The longterm aim should be to reduce very considerably the number of offenders who are detained in prison.

The urgent adoption of *Community Service Orders* is proposed at least for a trial period, until such time as comparisons of the rates of recidivism can be made. The Commission members are also impressed by the programme of Non-Institutional Care in Sweden where 'it is a widespread view and supported by experience that better preventive results are obtained at the individual level by correctional care outside institutions. Non-institutional care is also a more humane and a cheaper form of care than institutional'. (Fact-sheet of the Swedish information service abroad — *'Correctional Care in Sweden'*). Again the Commission is interested in the work of The *Shaftesbury Project in England,* the progress of *Community Service Orders in N.I.* (See 'Community Service Orders — N. Ireland Probation and After-Care Service) and the programme of reform advocated by Charles Colson's 'Prison Christian Fellowship' in the U.S.

Having examined all submissions made to it and having enquired into certain areas which were not adequately clarified in the submissions, the Commission wishes to propose a number of general and specific recommendations (in addition to the above mentioned Community Service Orders). The recommendations are made and published for the information of the public, in whose name our prison system operates, and for the attention of those who can put them into effect.

Part I: Structural Changes in the Penal System and Procedures

We have reviewed the changes in the treatment of offenders that have taken place — and that continue to take place — in a number of different countries where serious attempts are being made to deal with the questions of penal reform and rehabilitation. The problems involved are world wide and stem from a growing realisation that existing custodial prison systems do not rehabilitate offenders and are not effective deterrents. The rapid growth of urbanisation and of large population centres is also a contributing factor.

However, the whole question of penal reform and of the suitability of the existing prison system has been rendered more difficult in Ireland by reason of the very substantial number of political prisoners that have peopled Irish prisons. Paradoxically, the fact that a large proportion of our prison population has consisted of persons whose detention resulted from the political turmoil in the country has precluded an objective study of the adequacy or inadequacies of our penal system. Ever since the State was set up — and indeed, for some years before — the prime consideration of the prison service has been security and deterrence. Conversely, political parties or illegal organisations have used criticism of prison conditions as propaganda material. Because of these factors, less attention has been given in Ireland to penal reform than in most other developed countries. In addition, the Department of Justice and, indeed, successive Governments have been irrationally intolerant of criticism and of any constructive suggestions. Suggestions and criticisms alike were always regarded as ill-informed or subversive, if not both.

Within the prison population, the presence of a substantial number of prisoners claiming that their actions were politically motivated and justified inevitably damaged prison discipline and rendered the organisation of a prison system more difficult and controversial.

Prior to the setting up of the Free State and of the Republic, the prison system was controlled and administered by the Board of Prison Commissioners and the Visiting Committees that were appointed for each of the prisons. This system provided a measure of decentralisation and a greater measure of flexibility. The Board of Prison Commissioners disappeared, and their functions were vested in the Department of Justice. While Visiting Committees remained nominally in existence, their powers were greatly reduced and curtailed, and in many cases they ceased to exercise any effective supervision.

The entire control of the prison system, in effect, became vested in the officials of the Department of Justice; subject, of course, to the political direction of the Minister for Justice. The Ministers for Justice, as is inevitable in a democracy, have been transient. Few of them would ever claim that they were experts in social sciences, psychiatry, criminology, or in penal reform. They have to depend largely on the civil servants who run the Department of Justice to operate the prison system. Few, if any, of the officials of the Department of Justice have had any training in social science, psychology, education, or penal reform. They just happened to have been assigned to that particular department; they could just as easily have been assigned to any other department such as Posts and Telegraphs, or Local Government. The running of a penal system is a highly complex operation which does necessitate a personnel motivated and trained to deal with offenders and every aspect of their treatment and their rehabilitation.

Treatment of Offenders Board

Having given very careful consideration to the entire problem, the Commission recommends that the existing structures whereby the Department of Justice is invested with the sole and exclusive responsibility of dealing with prisons and prisoners should be recast.

The existing structures were the result of improvisations, resulting from reasons not related to penal reform or rehabilitation, to deal with different emergency situations. The entire responsibility for the treatment of offenders should instead be vested in a *Treatment of Offenders Board* consisting of not less than nine members and not more than eleven. Membership of the Board should not include more than two members from the existing Prison system

84

or Civil Service. The other members of the Board should be independent persons, appointed because of their expertise and experience in the fields of Education, Religion, Medicine, Social Sciences, Trade Unions, Business, or other relevant disciplines. The organisation under the control of the Treatment of Offenders Board should be divided under four separate divisions.

(i)   *The Security Division,* which would be assigned jointly to the Department of Justice and the Gardaí Síochána. This Division would have sole responsibility for the custodial containment of offenders and security related to the places of detention.

(ii) *The Rehabilitation Division.* This Division should occupy the central role in advising the Board as to the particular type of treatment to be provided for each individual offender. Its motivation should be the rehabilitation of each offender. This will involve the provision of education, training, remedial treatment, aftercare, and reintegration of offenders into society. Wherever reasonably possible, custodial detention should be avoided or reduced to a minimum. This Division should be under overall control of a Director chosen by reason of his or her training and experience in Social Work.

(iii) *Preventive Division.* This Division should analyse and keep under constant review the incidence and causes of juvenile delinquency. Where appropriate, it should consult with the educational and Gardaí authorities as to the incidence of different types of offences. The function of this Division should be to identify the underlying causes of offences and to initiate measures that could be taken to reduce the incidence of certain types of offences. Such measures might involve the provision of educational training facilities. The provision of social and sports activities to reduce the incidence of petty juvenile delinquency in built-up areas should be envisaged.

(iv) *Building, Maintenance, Catering and Administrative Division.* This Division should be responsible to the Board for the building, maintenance, catering and administration (including financial control) of all institutions under the control of the Board. This Division should be under the control of specialists in the different aspects of the administration.

Each of these four Divisions would report directly to the Treatment of Offenders Board. The Department of Justice would provide the administrative services for the Board, and would exercise supervisory functions on behalf of the Board. The Board would report directly to the Minister and consult with the Minister at regular intervals.

In addition to the Treatment of Offenders Board, there should be *Visiting Committees* for each prison that should work in close collaboration with the Probation and Welfare Officers attached to the Prison, and should be given direct access to the Board.

Visits by Judges to all prisons at regular intervals should be provided for and the visiting Judges should have direct access to the Board.

The Commission further recommends that the administration of prisons should be open to public scrutiny.

Pre-sentence reports should be provided on a much wider basis for the benefits of sentencing judges.

Part II: General Conclusions and Recommendations

In regard to the treatment of offenders, the primary objective should be the protection of society and the rehabilitation of the offender into society. Imprisonment or Institutionalised Custody should only be resorted to in cases which would represent a real danger to society. In all other cases, non-custodial methods should be used. The rate of recidivism among the prison population is one of the indications that imprisonment does not act as a deterrent.

Where a convicted person is imprisoned, the case should be kept under constant review to determine whether the offender still constitutes a threat to society or to any individual member of society.

The case of every offender serving a term of imprisonment should be reviewed at frequent intervals with a view to releasing the offender on parole for the unexpired portion of the sentence.

In the case of minor offences and particularly in the case of juvenile offenders, the Gardaí should be encouraged to caution the offenders and to refer them to probation officers, welfare officers, or to voluntary agencies that could provide hostel accommodation rather than to charge them and prosecute them in the District Courts. Such a referral system should be monitored by a responsible independent Ombudsman.

A system of appropriate community service should be organised so that, as an alternative to imprisonment, offenders could be ordered by the Courts to carry out specified community services for such number of days or hours as the Court might decide. Such *Community Service Orders* could also stipulate that the offender should reside at an appointed hostel in a given area.

Extensive provisions should be made for the setting up of supervised hostels, day centres, and employment schemes for offenders.

Orders of conditional discharge and binding-over orders should be used more frequently by the Courts.

Special bail hostels should be provided where an offender or suspected offender could be ordered to reside under supervision during the period of time that he is allowed out on bail.

Some detoxification centres should be provided in, at least, Dublin and Cork, which persons charged with drunkenness are free to attend as part of their sentence.

Judges should be given the power to impose sentences of detention or community service where they could be performed at weekends and during the periods of vacation or leave of the offender. From the time an order of imprisonment or community service is made in respect of an offender, the offender in question should be assigned to the care of a probation officer or a welfare officer whose function it would be to maintain contact with the offender's family, and to organise well in advance the provision of employment, and if necessary, housing, for the offender upon the completion of his or her sentence. Where no employment is readily available, in any given case, provision should be made to enable the offender to reside in an appointed hostel until such time as employment is available.

In the case of motoring offences, a system should be introduced whereby the offender would be required to attend classes at weekends as to the dangers which result from dangerous or careless driving. Special films should be available depicting the causes of accidents, and the offenders should be required to view these films.

Many of the juvenile offenders come from city areas wherein housing conditions are inadequate. Many also come from deprived families and from inadequate homes. It is suggested that small schools and social centres should be provided in these areas. The teachers for these schools should be specially trained and picked, and their aim should be to provide guidance and counsel to the juveniles attending their schools. Schools should be combined with small, social centres, under the care of social welfare officers who would work in close collaboration with the teachers. The aim of these centres should be to provide pleasant surroundings and occupational therapy for youngsters who otherwise would be roaming the streets. The help of voluntary organisations should be sought in the running of these small school-cum-social centres.

In the case of custodial sentences, provision should be made whereby the offender could be released on parole, every morning, to enable him or her to work during the day and to return during the evening. In the case of offenders who have no regular employment, the welfare officer to whom such an offender is entrusted should seek to obtain employment for the offender.

The Community Welfare Officers should visit the prisoner before his or her release to make sure he or she has money for food. If necessary a ticket should be issued for accommodation at a hostel and a referral note to his or her local CWO. If two weeks remission of sentence were given to each prisoner and the cost of those two weeks' keep given to him or her in the form of a voucher for food and lodgings, the immediate problems facing many ex-prisoners would be taken care of and making a new start would be more likely.

Persons on release should be given information as to the services provided by and the whereabouts of the relevant agencies: the Labour Exchange, the City Hostels, the nearest CWO., Manpower and the Local Health Centre.

Part III: Specific Recommendations on Health and Physical Conditions of Prisoners

The Commission notes the numerous representations made to it concerning the antiquity of buildings used for the containment of prisoners and urgently recommends the provision of modern toilet, recreational and educational facilities in all Irish prisons.

It is also recommended that the use of solitary confinement as a punishment be abolished forthwith.

Allegations concerning the abuse of drugs and medicines in Irish prisons should be examined by an independent agency.

The Department of Health should compile a comprehensive health programme for prisoners in all centres of detention.

In view of the strain imposed on the spouse and family of long-term prisoners, the Commission recommends that visits from family and friends should take place more frequently in more congenial surroundings than at present.

Detention of Juvenile Offenders

Juvenile offenders should never be detained in Garda Stations, or Bridewells. In Dublin and in Cork, special hostels should be provided to which juvenile offenders or suspects should be remanded before being brought to the District Courts. The period of detention before charging any juvenile suspect should be extended so as to enable qualified welfare officers to examine each individual case, and to prepare a full report for the District Justice.

While there have been considerable improvements in regard to the provision of educational and vocational training for juveniles who are in detention, a greater effort must continue to be made so as to ensure that each juvenile will receive the individual attention of qualified teachers and welfare officers.

The Commission recommends that the public statement of the Prison Officers' Association urging the closure of St. Patrick's Institution be given full consideration by the Government, or, failing closure, that school classes held there should not be closed during the summer vacation but that teachers be employed during the normal school vacations. A Certificate of Attainment from one of the teachers working in St. Patrick's has proved of value to former inmates seeking employment. The issuing of such certificates should be formally recognised by the Department of Education.

The Commission believes that the opening of Loughan House was a retrograde and wasteful measure. In the absence of evidence of its success to date, we favour much smaller custodial units, situated within reasonable visiting distance from the families and parents of those detained.

In future all places of detention for juveniles should be administered under the joint auspices of the Department of Education, Health and Justice, and never under the Department of Justice in the first instance.

Small non-custodial residential units with specially committed and experienced staff are considered more suitable for young offenders than large custodial institutions.

The age of criminal responsibility should be raised to fourteen years of age.

Detention of Females

The Commission notes the relatively low number of females in Irish prisons (daily average of 24 female inmates in 1979) and the relatively petty nature of most of the offences commited by those imprisoned. Therefore, it is recommended that the plans for a new women's prison should be cancelled.

A programme should be urgently undertaken to provide alternatives to prison for females who are convicted of petty offences.

Prostitution as a crime needs revision, in the opinion of the Commission. The law as presently applied appears unfair, as it favours men as against women. The Commission recommends that the law on Public Nuisance should be applied to the prostitute's clients as well as to the woman herself. The Commission is not at all convinced that imprisonment is a suitable manner of dealing with the social problem of female prostitution.

Prisoners' Rights

The Commission endorses prisoners' rights 'to form associations and unions' in accordance with Article 40, paragraph 6.1 of The Irish Constitution.

Members of minority religions should be free to practise the tenets of their faith regarding diet, due respect for the Sabbath, prayer-mats, etc.

Assistance from persons trained in law should be available to prisoners in the preparation and filing of legal actions.

Where principles of natural justice would appear to be infringed in such matters as punishment for breaches of prison discipline, the revocation of parole, etc., the final decision should be taken by an independent judicial officer. The accused has the right to be heard, to present evidence, and to cross-examine adverse witnesses, counsel being provided if of benefit to him or her.

Provision should be made in the Prison Rules for the exercise of their franchise by all inmates in local and national elections and referenda.

Prison Rules must comply with the standard minimum rules of the United Nations, and the recommendations of the U.N. Congress on the Prevention of Crime and the Treatment of Offences must be implemented. In particular the prison service must be recognised as 'an important social service demanding ability, appropriate training and good teamwork on the part of every member'.

The Prison Rules concerning the correspondence of prisoners should be improved to comply with the standard minimum rules of the European Convention on Human Rights.

The recommendations of the Ó Briain Committee

in relation to prisoners' rights should be implemented.

Rehabilitation into Society of Former Prisoners

The Commission notes the lack of effort made by the community in general to rehabilitate former prisoners into society and to prevent recidivism. Accordingly it makes the following recommendations:

A *Council for the Rehabilitation of Offenders* should be set up to promote and monitor the whole process of rehabilitative work, training and education in and out of detention. Trade Unions and Employer Organisations would form constituent bodies of such a council.

The State should take the initiative in providing employment for ex-prisoners.

The Trades Unions should be consulted by the Department of Justice on their attitude to prison labour, the Commission urges the formulation of a joint policy by these two.

Education of the general public regarding the problems and needs of prisoners is essential.

Prisoners should receive a training in various trades while serving their sentences.

Every person being released from prison should be given a letter stating the length of time served and the date of release, as the Labour Exchange demands to know these facts.

Persons released from the Central Mental Hospital should be referred to their local G.P. who should be informed of treatment administered while in the C.M.H.

Probation Officers, Community Workers, Social Workers, Welfare Officers, Gardaí and Voluntary Bodies should co-ordinate their social services.

Prisoners should not be discharged on bank-holiday week-ends or on Fridays when social services are not available.

Prison Staff and Personnel

The Commission notes the great demands imposed on prison officers and other personnel to provide an acceptable service to prisoners under their care today. Because of this demand the Commission recommends the following:

More extensive training for *Prison Officers* should be provided.

Greater liaison should take place between the universities and the criminal justice system. Universities could play a large part in research, in monitoring developments throughout the world, and in the training of police forces and of those concerned with prisons. The setting up of an *Irish Institute of Criminology* is recommended for the purpose of researching the many neglected but crucial questions which have been merely touched upon in this report.

Offenders should be supervised more closely by *Welfare Officers* who, through their involvement with individual offenders, might well be able to advise them about employment after sentence is served.

Chaplains and Medical Officers

Difficulties experienced by some *Prison Chaplains* and *Medical Officers* who, at times, feel a duality of loyalties, have been mentioned to the Commission and the view has been expressed that this duality might be relieved were the salaries of such officials paid through ecclesiastical and medical authorities rather than through the Department of Justice. The

Commission does not feel competent to comment on the practicalities of such an arrangement but urges that all possible steps be taken to ensure that clergy and doctors, who have responsibility for prisoners, feel completely free to follow the highest standards of their calling.

Preventive Measures

Across a wide spectrum of submissions which came from such sources as priests serving in disadvantaged areas, civil servants, prison-chaplains, social-workers (voluntary and professional) and peacegroups as well as some political parties, a uniform insistence was maintained on the correlation between offenders and disadvantaged socio-economic backgrounds. The Commission, although unwilling to ascribe poverty as an essential *cause* of crime, nevertheless cannot fail to recognise the prevailing background of poverty, unemployment and lack of education to be found in a large percentage of the inhabitants of our jails. Accordingly, the Commission recommends:

That a determined campaign against urban poverty be made so that the increasing stream of young offenders finding their way into prison be reduced.

That the Gardaí should have the assistance of social and welfare officers when serving in deprived urban areas.

That more hostels for adults and young people be set up in the Dublin area.

That there be positive discrimination for jobs in favour of inner-city children and that more teachers be employed in inner city schools.

That a nation-wide *Probation Service* be fully used and that institutional sentences be considered a last resort.

That educational standards, training and social skills of Gardaí be raised to enable them to become more expertly involved in community affairs. This will involve longer and broader training than at present available to members of the force.

That there should be a role for Gardaí involvement in planning new or renewed community projects so that possible problem areas in relation to crime may be recognised and avoided well in advance.

That financial and other support from voluntary and statutory sources be provided for the support of *Youth Work Programmes* designed to help the personal, social and cultural development of young people from less privileged urban areas.

That an independent *Police Authority* should be set up as well as an *Independent Tribunal* to examine complaints against the Gardaí, thus protecting the interests of both Gardaí and suspects in their custody.

The Curragh Military Detention Unit

The Commission recommends:

The closure of the Military Detention Unit at the Curragh — the only prison administered by military personnel in Europe. In recommending the closure of this Military Detention Units, the Commission is particularly impressed by the consistently expressed opinion of its Visiting Committee that this closure should be effected.

Abolition of the Death Penalty

The Commission agrees with the conclusions arrived at by Amnesty International (after a long and careful study of the question) that the death penalty should be totally abolished. Accordingly, we recommend that the death penalty be completely removed from Irish law.

Sínithe: *Seán Mac Bride*
Michael D. Higgins
Gemma Hussey
Michael Keating
Mary McAleese
Patrick McEntee
Mícheál Mac Gréil
Matt Merrigan
Muireann Ó Briain
Una O'Higgins O'Malley

Samhain 1980.

Submissions

SUBMISSIONS RECEIVED BY THE COMMISSION OF ENQUIRY INTO THE IRISH PENAL SYSTEM

A. Papers* and Reports to Public Hearing (6-8 April 1979)

1. "Rationale of Punishment" — Barry McAuley, Lecturer in Criminology, U.C.D.

2. "Parliamentarians, Prosecution and Prisons" . . — Mr Ciarán Mac An Aili, Solicitor

3. "The Irish Penal System — 1850 to 1950" . . . . — Mr Luke Gibbons, Researcher

4. "The Irish Criminal Justice System" . . . . — Mr Séamus Breathnach, Barrister

5. "The Women's Prison" . . . — Ms Máirín De Búrca, Journalist

6. "Military Custody" . . . . . . — Mr Patrick MacCartan, Solicitor

7. "Child Imprisonment" . . . . — Ms Mary Harding, Social Worker, Ms Paula Scully, Solicitor

8. "Open Prisons" . . . . — Mr Joe Costello, P.R.O.

9. "Prisoners Rights Through Legal Action" . . . . — U.C.D. Law Students Research Group

10. "Submission re Protection of Juveniles in Police Custody" . . . . — Michael D. White, Solicitor

11. "Scandinavian Penal System" . . . . — Mr Thomas Ekbom, Swedish Penologist

12. "The International Dimension — How Helpful

is it in Securing Prisoners'
Rights and Penal Reform in
Ireland?" . . . . Senator Mary Robinson
13. "Human Rights in Prison"   Walter Walsh, U.C.D.
14. "Loughan House" — A Survey of 50 12-15 year olds con-
    ducted by the *Prisoners Rights Organisation.*
15. *Case Histories of Ex-Prisoners:* The Commission was
    presented with the findings of a survey on 200 ex-prisoners
    with guest speakers and case histories.
16. "Administrative Law in Prisons", including Probation and
    Parole, Legal Advice, Specific Prisoners Rights such as the
    Right to Communicate, the right to Associate and the
    Right to Bodily Integrity.
17. "Towards Identification of Educational Priorities in
    Dublin" by Agnes Breathnach
18. "Criminal Neglect — Some Aspects of Law Enforcement
    as it Affects the Single Homeless" — the *Simon Community.*

*Papers were illustrated by ex-prisoners' submissions where relevant.

B. Group Submissions

1. The Irish Association of Social Workers
2. The Prison Fellowship Organisation, Mr Charles Colson
   and Mr G Loux.
3. The Association for Legal Justice
4. TRUST, A Medical and Social Service for Dublin's Home-
   less
5. PATCH, People Active Through Community Help
6. Irish Council for Civil Liberties
7. The Student Campaign Against Repression
8. Socialist Labour Party
9. PAX CHRISTI
10. The Combat Poverty Committee
11. Irish Civil Rights Action League
12. Probation and Welfare Officers
13. The Irish Republican Socialist Party
14. School Attendance Officers and Former Prison Officers
15. Local Government Public Services Union, Limerick
16. Simon Community

C. Submissions from Special Categories of Citizens:

1. Prison Chaplains, Priests and Religious (With special Sub-mission from Fathers Brian Power, Michael Sweetman SJ, John Brady, SJ and Piaras O Duill, OFM Cap)
2. Teachers and School Attendance Officer
3. Mothers of Boys in Loughan House
4. Solicitors
5. Ex-Prisoners of the Curragh Military Detention Unit
6. Social Workers
7. Wives of Prisoners

D. Papers were Received by the Commission Concerning

1. The Council of Europe Standard Minimum Rules for the Treatment of Prisoners
2. Declaration of the Hague
3. United Nations Minimum Rules
4. Habeas Corpus Act

Correspondence

TELEPHONE: DUBLIN 694225

ROM: SEAN MACBRIDE, S.C.

ROEBUCK HOUSE,
CLONSKEA,
DUBLIN 14
IREL⌐

His Excellency,
Deputy Gerry Collins
Minister for Justice
Government Buildings
Upper Merrion Street
Dublin 2

1 May 1980

Dear Minister,

As you are probably aware, following upon a Seminar organised
by the Prisoner's Rights Organisation in April 1979, which was
held at Milltown Park, a Commission to investigate problems
relating to our prison system and the treatment of offenders,
was set up. I append herewith a list of the members of the
Commission.

The Commission has been meeting systematically since it was set
up, and has received a considerable amount of oral and written
submissions.

We now hope to be in a position to consider our final conclusio⌐
before the end of next June.

Naturally, before considering our conclusions, we should like t⌐
have an opportunity of meeting you, and such senior officers of
your Department as you might wish to designate, to obtain the
benefit of your views and those of the Departmental Officers wh⌐
have been dealing with these problems.

ordingly, the Commission has asked me to ascertain whether
a would be prepared to meet the Commission, and to designate
he senior officials from your Department to meet the Commission.

you are agreable to this course, we can communicate further
rough your Secretary to decide on a convenient time for such
scussions.

Yours sincerely,

Sean MacBride, S.C.
Co-Chairman
Commission of Enquiry into
the Irish Penal System

7th May. 1980.

Dear Mr. MacBride,

I have your letter dated 1 May.

Perhaps you would let me know to whom your Commission is to report, wh
its terms of reference are and what precisely are the "problems" to wh
you refer.   I should also be interested in knowing what persons or bo
have given evidence and whomelse you have in mind to look for evidence

What kind of a meeting do you envisage?   Do you perceive it as being
measurable in weeks or merely in hours?   Would you envisage meeting,
example, basic grade prison staff and "specialists" such as welfare st
and teachers?

Yours sincerely,

Gerard Collins, T.D.,
MINISTER FOR JUSTICE

Mr. Sean MacBride, S.C.
Roebuck House,
Clonskea,
Dublin 14.

SEÁN MAC BRIDE, S.C.

ROEBUCK HOUSE,
CLONSKEA,
DUBLIN 14,
IRELAND.

His Excellency
Deputy Gerard Collins, T.D.
Minister for Justice
Government Buildings
2 St Stephen's Green
Dublin 2

19 May 1980

Dear Minister,

Many thanks for your letter of 7th May.

The Commission will in the first instance, address it's Report
to you, to the Minister for Health, the Minister for Education,
and to the Prisoners Rights Organisation. The terms of reference
of the Commission were as indicated in my letter of 1st May.

As to the problems to which the Commission has been addressing
itself; they are many and I feel certain they are already well-
known to you. They have frequently been discussed in the press
and have been the subject of many representations to the Government
and it's agencies from numerous non-governmental organisations.

In brief, the major problem is the escalation in offences being
committed in our society, the effectiveness or inadequacy of the
rehabilitation process, and in particular, the problems arising
from juvenile delinquency. There is, as you are no doubt aware,
some considerable doubt as to the effectiveness of existing
methods for dealing with offenders.

I shall arrange to have prepared a list of the persons and bodies
who have made submissions to the Commission, and I shall let you
have this as soon as possible.

At the moment, we are not contemplating inviting any other persons
to give evidence or make submissions to the Commission other than
your good self, the Commissioner of the Gardai, and such other
officials or Prison Staff as you might care to suggest.

As to the kind of meeting which we envisage, I do not expect it
would take more than half a day, or an evening. It would be for
the purpose of discussing with you informally and confidentially
possible remedies to the problems which undoubtedly exist. The

105

aim of the Commission is to try and find constructive solutions to some of the problems which exist; it is not the aim of the Commission to indulge in destructive criticism. Therefore, the Commission would greatly welcome any views or advice which you might be able to give to the Commission in regard to all, or any of the problems under consideration.

The Commission, I am sure, would also greatly welcome any suggestions which you might wish to make as to the possibility of meetings with Officials of the Department of Justice, Prison Staff, Welfare Staff, or Teachers.

The problems that exist in Ireland in regard to offences and treatment of offenders are by no means peculiar to Ireland; are pretty well generalised. Historical and political events have added some complications in our case.

I trust that the foregoing indication of the reasons why we w very much appreciate an opportunity to discuss these matters you will satisfy you as to the constructiveness of our approa and the desirability of the proposed discussions.

With warm best wishes,

Yours sincerely,

Seán MacBride

Sean MacBride, S.C.

s Excellency
>uty Gerard Collins, T.D.
nister for Justice
vernment Buildings
  St Stephen's Green
>lin 2   30 May 1930

ar Minister,

rther to my letter of 19 May, I now enclose a list of the
>missions made to the Commission of Enquiry into the Irish
al System.

 there is anything else you would like to know about our
rk, please do not hesitate to get in touch with me.

th best wishes,

                         Yours sincerely,

                         Seán MacBride

                         Sean MacBride, S.C.

OIFIG AN AIRE DLÍ AGUS CIR:
(Office of the Minister for Justice)
BAILE ÁTHA CLIATH
(Dublin)

25ᵗʰ June, 1980.

Dear Mr. MacBride,

I have your further letter.   I was interested in the information gi
by you in reply to my queries as to whom the commission is to report
and as to those who have given evidence.

I do not wish, by agreeing to any of your suggestions, to be put in
position of appearing to give some form of official approval for an
exercise prompted by the organisation referred to in your reply and
which the commission intends to report.

Yours sincerely,

Gerald Collins, T.D.,
MINISTER FOR JUSTICE

Sean MacBride, Esq., S.C.,
Roebuck House,
Clonskea,
Dublin 14.

AN GARDA SIOCHANA

Any reply to this communication should be addressed to:

Commissioner,
Garda Siochána,
Phoenix Park,
Dublin 8.

and the following number quoted:

OIFIG AN CHOIMISINEARA,

BAILE ÁTHA CLIATH.

13th May, 1980.

Sean McBride, S.C.,
Roebuck House,
Clonskea,
Dublin, 14.

Dear Mr. McBride,

I am in receipt of your letter of May 3, 1980 concerning your examination of the Irish Penal System.

As Commissioner of An Garda Siochana, with responsibility for Law enforcement, it does not fall within my area of competence to discuss or otherwise comment on the prison system and the treatment of prisoners.

Accordingly, I don't feel that it is appropriate that I or any of my Officers should attend, as requested in your letter.

Yours sincerely,

COMMISSIONER.

FROM: SEÁN MAC BRIDE, S.C.

Mr Patrick McLaughlin
Garda Commissioner
Headquarters
Phoenix Park
Dublin 8

ROEBUCK HOUSE,
CLONSKEA,
DUBLIN 14,
IRELAND.

19 May 1980

Dear Commissioner,

Very many thanks for your letter of 13 May.

I fully appreciate that the primary concern of An Garda Siochana
is that of Law Enforcement.   We felt, however, that related to
the questions of law enforcement there were a number of ancillary
matters that would be relevant and of interest to the Gardai.
Foremost among these are the measures which might be taken to
reduce the incidence of juvenile delinquency.   Another related
issue is the after-care of persons who have been released from
penitential detention.

Very few are really satisfied that our existing methods are adequate
to deal with the nature and extent of the problems that are a cause
of general concern.   The Commission felt that your views, and/or
those of experienced senior Garda Officers, would be of assistance
and value.   Needless to say, any discussion which might take place
would be regarded as informal and confidential.

I thought that I should put these additional views before you, but
shall fully understand if you continue to think that the discussions such as I have suggested would be inappropriate.

With warm best wishes,

Yours sincerely,

Seán MacBride. S.C.

110

Notes on Members

Chairman of Commission:

SEÁN MAC BRIDE: Senior Counsel at the Irish Bar, Former Minister for External Affairs; Secretary-General of the International Commission of Jurists; President of the International Peace Bureau, Geneva; Recipient of Nobel (1974) and Lenin (1977) Peace Prizes, and of the American Medal of Justice (1978)

Co-Chairman of Public Hearing (6-8 April-1979):

DR. LOUK HULSMAN: Professor of Criminology, University of Erasmus, Holland; Chairman of Committee on De-Criminalisation of the Council of Europe.

Members:

MICHAEL D. HIGGINS: Chairman of the Labour Party; Lecturer in Sociology, University College, Galway.

SENATOR GEMMA HUSSEY: Member of Seanad Éireann representing the National University of Ireland Constituency.

MICHAEL KEATING, T.D.: Fine Gael Spokesman on Human Rights and Law Reform; Former Member of Visiting Committee to St. Patrick's Institution (1974-'78).

DR. MARY MC ALEESE: Professor of Criminal

Law, Trinity College, Dublin; Member of Current Affairs Programming Staff of R.T.E.

PATRICK MC ENTEE: Senior Counsel at the Irish Bar.

DR. MÍCHEAL MAC GRÉIL, S.J.: Lecturer in Sociology, St. Patrick's College, Maynooth: Vice-President of National Youth Council of Ireland.

MATT MERRIGAN: General Secretary of Amalgamated Transport and General Workers Union; President of the Socialist Labour Party.

MUIREANN Ó BRIAIN: Barrister at Law; Secretary of the Association of Irish Jurists.

UNA O'HIGGINS O'MALLEY: Solicitor; Council Member of the Glencree Reconciliation Centre; Independent Human Rights Dail Candidate.

CAITRÍONA LAWLOR: Secretary of Commission.

PART II
POLICE CUSTODY AND
INTERROGATION

Police Custody and Interrogation
The Barra Ó Briain Committee Report; its History and Importance

Kevin T. White, Chairman, Irish Section of Amnesty International

The Irish Government had a glorious opportunity in the late 1970s to establish in this country a practical example of how International Conventions on Human Rights could be put into practical effect in a democratic society. Amnesty International's findings of ill-treatment of suspects by Gardai in 1977 led to an official inquiry into safeguards for people in custody — and for protecting the good name of the Gardai. As Amnesty's then General Secretary told the Minister for Justice at the time, it was an unique opportunity to set an example of world-wide significance.

Unfortunately, the opportunity was missed. The politicians chose inaction, deflecting the real issues with deceptive public statements. The only meaningful recommendations of the Ó Briain Committee were rejected. Ireland, it appeared, had no intention of becoming a model for the protection of prisoners and human rights generally.

Amnesty sent a mission to Ireland in June 1977 as a result of a steady stream of complaints that suspects were being maltreated while in Garda custody. The mission found enough evidence for it to conclude that maltreatment appeared to have occurred in a number of cases while suspects were under interrogation. Carried out by detectives specialising in serious, politically-motivated crimes it was intended to secure incriminating statements. In addition the mission found that the Special Criminal Court had seemingly failed or refused to scrutinise allegations of ill-treatment.

The mission's report was followed up with a submission to the Government in August 1977 expressing concern at the findings and at the fact that the Government authorities had not seen fit to investigate them impartially. The United Nations Declaration of 9th December 1975 protecting people from torture and inhuman treatment requires investigation of such allegations — whether a formal complaint is made or not. The Coalition Government, in power until June 1977, had refused an impartial inquiry as requested by Amnesty International and insisted that such allegations could be dealt with only by the Courts. The newly elected Fianna Fáil Government adopted a somewhat broader approach. It set up the Committee headed by Judge Barra Ó Briain in October 1977. The other members were a former Garda Commissioner, Patrick Malone, and the General Secretary of the Irish Congress of Trade Unions, Ruaidhri Roberts.

The Committee was charged with recommending safeguards for people in custody and for the protection of Gardai against unjustified allegations. It was excluded from investigating allegations, although it could and did consider Amnesty's findings as the basis for its work.

At the same time, the Government announced the secondment of a senior Garda officer to help with the inquiries into past allegations of ill-treatment. It became clear that the Government's view on investigating these cases was precisely the same as that of its predecessor, i.e. the allegations could only be examined in the context of the legal system by charging the accused Gardai and bringing them before the Courts to answer accusations of criminal offences.

Effectively, the move confused public opinion by appearing, initially, to set up a special method of investigating the widespread allegations current during the previous years. But there was nothing very special about the arrangement. The main point at the end of the day was simply that the allegations were never investigated as the United Nations Declaration required.

Amnesty, in a letter to the Minister, regretted that the O Briain Committee had not been asked to investigate specific cases of alleged maltreatment. Nevertheless it welcomed the formation of the Committee and co-operated fully with it. It made written representations and two senior members of Amnesty spent a day making oral submissions to the Committee. After hearing submissions from a wide range of interested bodies, including the Garda Commissioner, Edmund Garvey, all four Garda Representative Bodies, and the Lawyers' Organisations, the Committee presented its findings to the Government in April 1978. The report was published the following October.

A central and all-important plank of the report was the comment that 80 per cent of people convicted for serious crimes were convicted on the basis of 'confessions'. A very high proportion of convicted people, in other words, were alleged to have incriminated themselves voluntarily. The Committee thought it unusual that there should be such a

117

heavy emphasis on confessions at the expense of other forms of police inquiry which they said seemed to indicate an inability or reluctance to secure evidence by scientific methods of criminal investigation and by persevering with police enquiries.

This point was central to the Committee's subsequent recommendations. Practically all of their suggestions hinged on it and indeed it seems to have proved to the satisfaction of the members that the need for safeguarding people in police custody was well founded.

Amnesty welcomed the report and found its recommendations to be 'constructive proposals for effective safeguards'. Minister for Justice Collins appeared equally warm towards them. The Government, he announced, had decided to accept the proposals. But he added a vital sub-clause: the acceptance was subject to a number of *'reservations and exceptions'*.

And he went on to list at considerable length a litany of reservations and exceptions. Recommendations were rejected as 'unacceptable', 'impracticable', 'requiring further examination' and needing 'careful consideration'. After all the reservations were added up, the report had been emasculated. All the significant and potentially effective proposals were smothered in verbal obfuscation.

The workmanlike report of Judge Ó Briain and his colleagues contains no radical proposals. But it sets out a series of measures which would go a long way towards resolving the basic problems of protecting people in custody and protecting the Gardai themselves from unfounded accusations. Unfortunately, the authorities seem to have overlooked the importance of the proposals for protecting the police

118

force itself. The atmosphere of recrimination and mistrust of the Garda Siochana which developed over the period investigated by Amnesty did not do the force or its individual members any good. It is unfortunate that the Garda Representative Associations should have allowed a feeling of defensiveness to blind them to the merits of the proposals for protection of their own members. Indeed it is noteworthy that throughout all Amnesty's investigations, in different parts of the world, of complaints similar to those which were the subject of the mission to Ireland, and upon which Amnesty has published reports, there runs a consistent pattern of methods used by police interrogation officers.

Of all the processes in the administration of justice, pretrial procedures can be vital to a person suspected of a crime. It must never be overlooked that the purpose of pretrial investigation is to ensure that justice is done, and is seen to be done, and is not merely for the purposes of making someone amenable for the alleged crime.

It has been the experience of Amnesty International that it is in the period of the pretrial investigations, i.e. during interrogation of suspects or, as it has come to be described, when persons are 'helping the police with their enquiries', that the greatest deprivations of human rights are likely to occur. It is therefore of the utmost importance that persons who 'are asked to assist the police with their enquiries' should be aware of their rights and of the obligations which rest upon the police in this regard. The task of the police in investigating crime is often frustrating and they are under pressure, particularly in these days when major crime is so prevalent, to get results, to get convictions, to make the statistics look good. This can lead to the temptation to cut corners in order to get confessions and so 'wrap up' a case — therein lies the danger to the citizen. Never should public dissatisfaction with escalating crime allow a climate to develop where the interest of the State — sometimes described as upholding law and order — is used to seek to justify the abrogation of the rights of the citizen.

The responsibility of Governments in this area, however, is not merely a pragmatic matter of ensuring that police forces do have the respect and acceptance of their citizens. Neither is it a purely domestic affair — as all the most ruthless dictatorships regularly claim — but a matter of international responsibility.

The United Nations General Assembly Declaration of 9th December 1975 condemns any act of torture or other cruel, inhuman or degrading treatment as 'an offence to human dignity'. Under its terms no State may permit or tolerate torture or other inhuman or degrading treatment and each State is requested to take effective measures to prevent such treatment from being practised within its jurisdiction.

Article 1 of the Declaration defines torture as 'any act by which severe pain or suffering, whether physical or mental, is intentionally inflicted by or at the instigation of a public official on a person for such purposes as obtaining from him or a third person information or confession'.

Article 9 of the Declaration provides that 'wherever there is reasonable ground to believe that an act of torture as defined in Article 1 has been committed, the competent authorities of the State concerned shall promptly proceed to an impartial investigation *even if there has been no formal complaint*'.

The temptation to law enforcement officers to ignore the legal safeguards for citizens always increases when crime becomes more prevalent and policemen come under greater pressure to obtain convictions. Needless to say, it is a temptation that must be resisted.

Implementation of the Ó Briain Committee's recommendations would go some way towards countering such temptations. Since Amnesty investigated the situation in Ireland in 1977, there appears to have been an improvement in the treatment of suspects in custody. But constant vigilance is needed to protect human rights against the systematic use of ill-treatment by police and against isolated cases where individuals are treated brutally.

The Ó Briain report's recommendations are the handiest measures available to balance the protection of rights against the temptations that may afflict policemen. They should be implemented immediately and become a permanent part of police practices in Ireland. The unequivocal commitment by the Government elected in July 1981, i.e. — 'the findings of the Ó Briain Committee will be implemented', was a welcome development. But up to the time of writing no attempt had been made to implement that commitment. Time is running out. Concern at the escalation of crime is widely voiced. Public spokesmen have indicated that there is a lack of community co-operation with the police and suggested that this stems from mistrust of Garda methods. The obvious way to dispel that mistrust and to restore public confidence is to implement the Ó Briain Committee recommendations without delay.

THE BARRA Ó BRIAN
REPORT

COMMITTEE TO RECOMMEND CERTAIN SAFEGUARDS FOR PERSONS IN CUSTODY AND FOR MEMBERS OF AN GARDA SÍOCHÁNA

To: An Taoiseach and other Members of the Government.

Introduction

1. On the 6th day of October, 1977, this Committee was appointed by Order of the Government. Mr. Justice Barra Ó Briain was nominated Chairman of the Committee, and Dr. Ruaidhri Roberts, General Secretary of the Irish Congress of Trade Unions, and Mr. Patrick Malone, former Commissioner of the Garda Síochána were nominated as members, Mr. Gerard Frewen B.L., a Registrar of the High Court being appointed Secretary to the Committee.

2. The Terms of Reference of the Committee were 'to recommend with all convenient speed whether, and if so, what additional safeguards are necessary or desirable for the protection against ill-treatment of persons in Garda custody, having regard to allegations made in relation to persons held in such custody pursuant to section 30 of the Offences Against the State Act, 1939, or section 2 of the Emergency Powers Act, 1976, and for the protection of members of the Garda Síochána against unjustified allegations of such ill-treatment; and for that purpose to seek

such information as would be likely to be of assistance to them in making a recommendation as aforesaid. The proceedings of the Committee will be private and their report will be made to the Government'.

3. The Committee decided at its first meeting:

(a) to invite any person or association of persons wishing to make submissions to the Committee to forward such submissions in brief written form, such written submissions to be furnished on or before the 18th November, 1977; a list of the organisations and persons specifically invited by letter to make submissions is given in Appendix A; and

(b) to invite such person or association of persons, if it seemed appropriate to the Committee, to elaborate on the written submissions at an oral hearing.

4. Advertisements to this effect were placed in the four national daily newspapers between the 28th October, 1977, and the 1st November, 1977.

5. Written submissions were received from nine organisations and from nine individuals or groups of individuals. These are listed in Appendix B. In addition, a dossier of statements and copy affidavits was submitted by Father Piaras Ó Duill, O.F.M.Cap., containing allegations by twenty-six persons of ill-treatment at the hands of the Gardaí.

6. Oral hearings were accorded to eleven organisations or groups of individuals. These are listed in Appendix C.

7. The Committee gratefully acknowledge the assistance and co-operation afforded us by the following who supplied material on request:

The Department of Foreign Affairs;

The Australian Embassy;

Miss Gleeson, Law Librarian, Trinity College, Dublin;

Mr. Gavan-Duffy, Librarian, Law Society, Dublin;

Miss Madill, Assistant Librarian, Queen's University, Belfast;

The Hon. Mr. Justice Walsh, President of the Law Reform Commission.

We also express our appreciation of the assistance given by those individuals who wrote to us but who were not called upon to make oral submissions.

8. We cannot praise too highly the assistance our Secretary Mr. Gerard Frewen, B.L. has given us. It is not too much to say that without the work he put into the organising of the Committee, the research and the processing of material which he undertook, as well as the arranging of meetings to suit the convenience of all the parties concerned, the Committee cold hardly have discharged its task. We are most grateful to him.

The Problem

9. Our Terms of Reference specifically required our recommendations to relate to allegations. The Committee decided to take the allegations contained in the Report of Amnesty International sent to the Taoiseach on the 26th August, 1977, and in the dossier supplied by Father Piaras Ó Duill, as representing whatever case could be made against the Garda Síochána, and on which might be based appropriate recommendations of suitable safeguards for the protection of persons in police custody in the future. Upon enquiry from Amnesty International we were informed that thirteen of the complainants in the Ó Duill dossier were among those whose cases were considered by the Amnesty International team when

it visited this country.

10. The Committee were at all times very conscious of the two-fold nature of our Terms of Reference. The protection of Gardaí from false allegations of ill-treatment is a highly desirable thing. We gave thought to the possibility of curtailing the "privilege" which attaches to allegations made in the Courts. However, we came to the conclusion that protection of persons in Garda custody and protection of Gardaí from false allegations are two sides of the same coin. The general view of those whom we heard, and our own conclusion, was that the more difficult it is made for police to ill-treat persons in their custody, the more difficult it will be successfully to fabricate charges of ill-treatment against the Gardaí. Out of Court allegations can, of course, be dealt with by the existing law of defamation.

Consideration of the Problem

11. In approaching its task the Committee was faced with alternate interpretations of its Terms of Reference. The narrow approach would restrict our deliberations to a consideration of subversive crime, particularly in the context of the Offences Against the State Act, 1939, (section 2 of the Emergency Powers Act, 1976 not having been continued in force by the Government). The broader interpretation of our Terms of Reference reasoned that if it had been the intention of the Government to limit our deliberations to the subversive field, this would have been expressly spelled out.

12. The Committee approached the question of interpretation with an open mind. It soon became quite evident that the majority of submissions from

all sides favoured the broad approach. Indeed, of the eleven groups which appeared before us, not one argued in favour of the narrow approach, and the great majority argued very strongly for the broad interpretation. It was accordingly decided unanimously by the Committee that this latter should be our approach to the problem.

13. There are at present 699 Garda Stations in the Republic, many of them open on a permanent basis. The Garda Síochána numbers approximately 9,000 members. For administrative purposes the country is divided into 21 Divisions, each under the control of a Chief Superintendent. Each division is subdivided into districts, and there are 103 Districts, each under the control of a Superintendent.

14. The primary function of a Garda has been described as the maintenance of law and order and the protection of the person and property of the general public. 'Law and order' is a dual concept and not a single idea. Problems inevitably arise when it becomes the function of the law to retain the official who has been appointed to keep order. The Garda, no less than any other citizen, is amenable to the law, and if the force to which he belongs is to retain public confidence he must be clearly seen to be so.

15. Fundamental to all considerations of arrest, questioning and allegations of ill-treatment is a consideration of the events which normally bring members of the public into contact with Gardaí investigating a crime. In our democratic society people have a right to liberty. Article 40.4.1° of the Constitution reads: 'No citizen shall be deprived of his personal liberty save in accordance with law'. People are therefore entitled to move freely, and their liberty may be interfered with only in accordance

with law, that is, when specifically authorised by Common Law or by Act of Parliament. A Garda investigating a crime, or indeed acting in the belief that a crime may have been committed, is entitled to ask questions of any person or persons, whether suspected or not, from whom he thinks that useful information may be obtained. There is no absolute obligation on the person being questioned to answer any question put to him, subject to a few well-defined statutory exceptions. Most persons, however, will give answers to a Garda when questioned. It may be embarrassing to the person to be accosted by a Garda at his place of employment or in his home, and he may voluntarily agree to go to a Garda Station to answer questions or to make a statement.

16. In the light of whatever answers he has received when questioning a member of the general public, a Garda is faced with deciding whether or not to pursue the questioning. It may be that the questioning takes place on the street, in a person's place of employment, or in his home. In many cases the Garda will 'invite' the person to accompany him to the station 'to assist him with his enquiries'. The person may agree to do this and the visit to the Station may be deemed to be voluntary i.e. there is no arrest at this stage. When the question and answer session has arrived at a stage where the Garda can reasonably be expected to have made up his mind to charge the person with a crime, he is required under the Judges' Rules (hereinafter mentioned in paragraph 27 and set out in full in Appendix D) to administer a formal 'caution' advising the person that from that moment on he is not legally obliged to answer any questions, and that any answers he may give will be taken down in writing and may be given in evidence.

17. The case may arise, and it not infrequently does, that a person reasonably suspected of having committed a crime and whom the Garda wishes to question may refuse to answer, or to accept the 'invitation' to go to the Garda Station. The Garda must now decide whether to allow the person to go his way unhindered or to arrest him. By arresting him he can compel the person to accompany him to the Station, using only such force or restraint as is necessary to achieve that end.

18. In making an arrest the Garda commits himself formally to a course of action which may have serious legal consequences not only for the person arrested but also for the Garda himself. In certain circumstances the Garda may face a civil action for false imprisonment. It will be readily understood, therefore, if Gardaí prefer to invite persons to come to the Station rather than to arrest them. Because of the dilemma facing the Garda in such a situation, the practice has grown over the years to secure 'voluntary' attendance at Stations by refraining from advising the 'invitees' of the legal realities of the situation. We believe that most people who go to Garda Stations to 'assist the police with their enquiries' do so under the misapprehension that they have no other choice than to do so. This practice has been condoned and as a result has become the established norm.

19. The acid test of whether a person is in a Garda Station as a mere invitee or is under some form of restraint, real or imagined, must surely be whether the person believes that he is free to walk out the door at any time he wishes to do so. If he is under any misapprehension or does not fully understand his rights in the matter, a Court might hold that he had been kept in custody.

20. It is the general law of this country, subject to a few statutory exceptions, that a grave duty rests on the Garda Síochána to bring an arrested person before a District Justice or a Peace Commissioner as soon after arrest as is conveniently possible.

21. The case of *Dunne v. Clinton* 1930 IR 366 highlighted the rejection by our Courts of a concept of detention short of actual arrest, the purpose of which was to enable the police to pursue enquires and to gather evidence. This decision was cited with approval in the case of *The People v. Stenson* (as yet unreported) in which Finlay, President, delivered the judgment of the Special Criminal Court on the 28th January, 1977.

22. The train of events in an arrest will vary with circumstances but the general pattern is as follows:— No more force than is reasonably necessary may be used in effecting the arrest. The clothing and property in the immediate possession of a person arrested on a criminal charge may be lawfully searched if the Garda has reasonable grounds for believing that he has a concealed weapon or implement, or to secure or preserve evidence connected with the offence for which he is being arrested. Unless the person is likely to dispose of articles suspected of being stolen by dropping them en route to the Station, or is believed to be in possession of a dangerous weapon, he is customarily not searched until brought to the Station.

23. Upon arrival at the Garda Station the arrested person is asked to furnish details for entry in the Station records. Thereafter he is administratively deemed by the Gardaí to be in the custody of the Station Orderly or of the member in charge for the time being in the Station. He may be lodged in a cell or other secure room in the Station. He may be

questioned about a crime or crimes other than that with which he has been charged. We believe that it has been the practice to question him, after arrest and before formal charge, not only about other crimes but also about the crime for which he has been arrested. Depending on the answers he gives, he may be invited to make a statement, a formal caution as provided in Rule 5 of the Judges' Rules (see Appendix D) having first been administered. The requirement is that a statement be voluntary, and it goes without saying that ill-treatment, whether physical or psychological, is absolutely forbidden.

24. All persons in custody are entitled, pursuant to Garda Regulations and provided that it is reasonable and practicable, to certain facilities. These are:

(a) the right to have his solicitor, and a member of his family or a friend, informed that he has been taken into custody;

(b) the right to receive a visit from, and consult privately with, his solicitor;

(c) the right to receive a visit from a member of his family or a friend, provided that such visit is not considered prejudicial to the interests of justice, and is supervised by a member of the Garda Síochána;

(d) provision, free of charge, of ordinary meals, or of meals of his own choice at his own choice at his own expense if it be practicable; and

(e) the right to be informed that he is entitled to communicate ·with his family, friend, legal or medical adviser, or to send for a bailsman.

The exercise of the foregoing rights may be by telephone, subject to supervision by a Garda to ensure that the call will not be used to prejudice the interests of justice. Oral or written communication may be used, subject to the same proviso.

25. It was held by the Court of Criminal Appeal in the case of *The Director of Public Prosecutions v Madden and others* (in which judgment was delivered by O'Higgins, Chief Justice, on the 16th November 1976, as yet unreported) that a person held in detention '. . . has got a right of reasonable access to his legal advisers, and that a refusal, upon request, to give such reasonable access would render his detention illegal. "Reasonable" in this context must, of course, be construed having regard to all the circumstances of each individual case, particularly as to the time at which access is requested, and the availability of the legal adviser or advisers sought'.

26. By a direction issued from the Office of the Commissioner of the Garda Síochána on the 7th November, 1973, copies of a Notice outlining the rights of persons taken into custody were required (a) to be displayed in a prominent position in charge rooms, public offices, waiting rooms and cell passages; and (b) to be handed to each person in custody by the arresting member of the force. We are satisfied that this direction has not been complied with in a number of instances. A copy of the Notice referred to is given in Appendix E.

27. Questioning of a suspected person is conducted, theoretically at least, in accordance with the Judges' Rules (previously referred to in paragraph 16 and set out in full in Appendix D). These rules were drawn up by members of the English Judiciary at the request of the British Home Secretary. The Rules did not purport to have the force of law, but were '. . . administrative directions, the observance of which the police authorities should enforce on their subordinates

134

as tending to the fair administration of justice'. The first set of Judges' Rules, four in number, was drawn up in 1912. In 1918 the Rules were revised and increased to nine in number; it is this set of Rules which is currently applied in this country.

28. Recent law in England has held that there can be a legal detention by police not amounting to arrest, but entitling the police to detain a suspect '. . . for so long as might be necessary to confirm their general suspicions or to show them to be unfounded'. This was the case of *Regina v. Brown* 1977 R.T.R. 160. This notional distinction between detention and arrest is entirely unknown to Irish law. In the case of *Dunne v. Clinton* previously referred to, Mr. Justice Hanna clearly stated 'In law there can be no half-way house between the liberty of the subject unfettered by restraint, and an arrest'. (1930 IR 372).

29. From our enquiries in the matter we are satisfied that the idea of 'detention', as distinct from 'arrest', has been notionally accepted and acted upon by some members of the Garda Síochána, and further, that some persons brought to Garda Stations for questioning have erroneously believed themselves to be under detention and not free to leave at will or free to refuse to answer questions. It is recognised at common law that after a person has been charged with an offence he is not obliged to make a statement and ought not to be questioned further about the offence by the police. In Irish law this prohibition on questioning would operate from the moment a person is taken into custody.

30. The way in which questioning of an arrested person is conducted depends on a variety of factors. In many cases only one officer will question. We are informed that this method has been found highly

effective where the questioning officer is able to establish a rapport with the subject, and by treating him humanely and sympathetically to draw from him the answers likely to lead to solution of the offence under investigation. In other cases two or more officers may participate in a questioning. This is more likely to occur when the person is an habitual criminal, well-versed in the practices of police questioning and his own legal and constitutional rights.

31. The place in which questioning will be carried out likewise depends on a number of factors. In most cases arrested persons will be brought to the nearest Garda Station. Facilities for questioning and imprisoning vary widely throughout the country. Some Stations, such as the Dublin Bridewell, are said to be equipped with adequate facilities for both. Other Stations do not have adequate facilities, or are dependent on primitive and degrading facilities.

32. The exercise by arrested persons of the right of access to a Solicitor seems to have received less than the wholehearted co-operation of the Gardaí. It appears that investigating officers frequently feel that the inevitable consequence of allowing a suspect access to a Solicitor will be a direction to the client/suspect to say nothing in reply to Garda questions. The judements of the American Supreme Court in *Escobedo v. Illinois* 378 U.S. 478 (1964) and *Miranda v. Arizona* 384 U.S. 436 (1966) indicate that the problem is a real and ubiquitous one. The revision of the Judges' Rules carried out in England in 1964 gives express recognition in that country to the problem and to the police difficulty when it says in Appendix A to the revised Rules 'Every person at any stage of an investigation should be able to communicate and to consult privately with a solicitor. This is so even if he is in

custody provided that in such a case no unreasonable delay or hindrance is caused to the process of investigation or the administration of justice by his doing so'. The words which we have underlined indicate the possibility of the police fear being justified i.e. that the introduction of a solicitor will tend to hinder what they regard as the process of investigation.

33. Whatever may be the rights of an arrested person in England, it is abundantly clear that his Irish counterpart has a right of access subject only to considerations of what is 'reasonable'. In his judgment on a habeas corpus application by one Noel Harrington delivered on the 14th December, 1976, Finlay, President of the High Court quoted with approval the words of O'Higgins, Chief Justice, which we have previously cited in paragraph 25. Finlay P. went on to define the procedure as access '. . . in privacy and out of the hearing of any member of the Garda Síochána'. It is a right exercisable not alone by the person in custody, but also by persons who have made a bona fide request for it on his behalf.

34. Heretofore, consideration has been given to arrest and questioning in regard to breaches of the law generally. The growth in the subversive crime rate has reached alarming proportions in recent years. There are aspects of subversive crime which, in practice, tend to attract to its investigation considerations which do not apply to 'ordinary' crime, and inevitably bring to it an emotive counter-reaction.

35. The State has recognised the peculiar difficulties of the Garda role in containing and defeating the subversive criminal, by conferring exceptional powers on the force under statute. The two most important statutes in this field are the Offences Against the State Act, 1939, and the Emergency Powers Act,

137

1976. The latter, as of the present moment, has not been renewed, but it can be brought into force at any time by Government Order. The 1939 Act empowers the Gardaí to arrest and detain for up to 48 hours, to require a true account of a suspect's movements, to search, photograph and take fingerprints. The exercise of these exceptional powers by the Gardaí in the subversive field has led, we believe, to much of the present apprehension on the part of the public and of the news media.

36. In a situation where nine thousand Gardaí exercise police powers daily in our community, it is inevitable that complaints will be made by members of the public against members of the Garda Síochána. At present, investigation of complaints is carried out by a senior officer of the Garda Síochána. Where the complaint involves merely a breach of discipline it will be dealt with by the Garda Commissioner. If a breach of the criminal law is disclosed, the matter will be passed to the Director of Public Prosecutions, who will decide whether or not to prosecute the offending Garda. Criticisms of the present system made to us suggested that it was slow, that it tended to deter most complainants, and that it was manifestly unfair in that it depended on investigation carried out by members of the force who might be less than willing to find fault in the behaviour of a colleague. On the other hand it was argued that most other professional bodies investigate complaints against their own members, that the Garda Síochána was better equipped than any other body to carry out the necessary investigation, and that if improved machinery was required for the investigation of complaints it could be created within the force. The Committee considered the operation of Complaints Review Bodies in England,

Northern Ireland and New York. The First Interim Report of the Australian Law Reform Commission on 'Complaints Against Police' was also considered.

37. We understand that it is a general complaint that where accusations are made against individual members of police forces, there is a tendency on the part of policemen not to co-operate wholeheartedly in the subsequent investigation of the complaint. This may be due to an understandable reluctance to becoming involved as a witness against a colleague. The 'wall of silence' which meets the investigating officers may well make any proper enquiry abortive. There may also arise the added difficulty of cases where the identity of the officer against whom it is sought to make complaint is unknown and unascertainable by the complaining member of the public. If the public has any ground to suspect that there is a 'cover-up', it is inevitable that a loss of public confidence in the force will ensue.

38. Statistics can be misleading and we would not wish to attach undue significance to the figures quoted to us. However, the statement that 80% of serious crimes, in respect of which convictions are obtained, are solved by confessions i.e. as the end-product of questioning sessions — seems to indicate a high degree of reliance on self-incrimination, and an inability or reluctance to secure evidence by scientific methods of criminal investigation and by persevering police enquiries.

39. One of the submissions made to the Committee was that the Prosecution be required to declare, on the first occasion an accused appears before a Court, whether a statement or confession made by the accused will be relied upon.

40. The desirability of securing the attendance of

a Third Party during the questioning of a person in custody was stressed again and again by delegates appearing before us. Consideration was given to various categories of person who would meet the requirements of a suitable Third Party. We finally concluded that the most suitable candidate would be a solicitor, preferably one of the person's own choosing. It was suggested to us that it was entirely feasible that a scheme be devised, in co-operation with the legal profession, whereby a panel of 'duty solicitors' might be maintained on a continuous basis. A solicitor on call for the period would be required to attend at a Garda Station upon request of a person in custody.

41. Nothing that we heard gave any ground for suspecting that Garda questioning was ever done through sadism or for purposes of graft. At worst it was suggested that the purpose of the questioning was to extract confessions of guilt, or to obtain information concerning the criminal activities of third parties. The problem has arisen that the Gardaí carry out questioning in many cases only because persons who are brought to Garda Stations fail, either through ignorance of their rights or fear of the Gardaí, to exercise their rights.

42. It is our conclusion that this represents a most unsatisfactory state of affairs both for the Garda Síochána and for persons brought to Garda Stations. The practice of detaining persons for the purpose of questioning them has no justification in law, apart from the exceptional cases provided for in 'Emergency' legislation. We feel that this form of detention should be terminated forthwith.

43. Legal authority exists at present for detention for the purposes of questioning under the 'Emergency'

legislation referred to in the preceding paragraph. The question was canvassed before us as to whether it was now time to extend that right to other cases, subject to stringent safeguards to prevent abuse. It was argued that serious crime can be just as disruptive of society and the State as so-called 'subversive' crime. Counterarguments were put to us to the effect that giving the power to detain for questioning leads inevitably to an over-reliance on that power to the exclusion of other methods of enquiry not involving any interference with the freedom of the individual. It was said that if a self-incriminating statement is regarded as essential evidence for obtaining a conviction, it creates a temptation to ill-treat a person detained, with a view to securing a statement in the appropriate terms; that the normal method of enquiry should not be to seek self-incrimination. Finally, it was argued that it is the use of the power to detain for questioning, given by 'Emergency' legislation, that has led to the allegations of ill-treatment which gave rise to the present enquiry, and that the fact that detention for questioning occurs without legal authority provides no basis for giving it legal authority.

44. Whether the arguments we have set out in the preceding paragraph, for and against the extension of the power of detention for questioning, are comprehensive or not, a further question has been raised as to whether any recommendation to this effect would be within this Committee's Terms of Reference. It is argued, in support of the view that it is not within our Terms of Reference, that freedom from detention is the best safeguard of all against the possibility of ill-treatment in detention, and as our Terms of Reference are concerned with the prevention of ill-treatment of persons in custody we can make no

recommendation for an extension of the circumstances in which a person can be taken into custody. Additionally it is argued that the issues involved, relating to the liberty of the citizen and the right of silence, are fundamental questions which could not be fully examined in the course of our enquiries. On these grounds — the Chairman dissenting — we considered that no recommendation could be made on the subject.

45. We now proceed to the making of specific recommendations for the provision of additional safeguards for the protection against ill-treatment of persons in Garda custody. As we said in paragraph 10, we are of the opinion that the matter of protection of members of the Garda Síochána against unjustified allegations of ill-treatment is but the other side of the same coin. In making recommendations regarding the protection of persons in custody, we believe that we are helping to protect the Gardaí from unjustified allegations.

Recommendations

46. The practice of taking people whom it is desired to question to a Garda Station 'to help the police with their enquiries' should be discontinued. We so recommend.

47. Where a person is arrested and brought to a Garda Station he should have assigned to him, on arrival in the Station, a member of the force who is not connected with the investigation or other police action which led to the arrest. For convenience this Garda is hereinafter referred to as the 'Custodial Guardian'. It would be the duty of the Custodial Guardian to ensure that the person is treated human-

ely and in strict accordance with Garda Regulations while he is in custody. Assignment of the Custodial Guardian should be made by the Station Sergeant or senior Garda then present in the Station. Once appointed he should be responsible, until officially relieved, for the well-being of the person in custody and the safe-guarding of his rights. The Custodial Guardian should immediately hand him the official printed form notifying him of his rights (Garda Form C 72 (S), a copy of which is set forth in Appendix E). He should satisfy himself as to whether the person requires medical examination, and if of opinion that it is necessary or desirable, he should have authority to prevent any questioning until a medical examination has been completed. In the case of an uninformed or illiterate person he should particularly ensure that he fully understands his rights. We so recommend.

48. It should be the duty of the Custodial Guardian to ensure that reasonable requests made by the person in custody are met, so far as possible. He should keep him informed as to progress in efforts to contact his solicitor, his family or friend. He should ensure that the person is afforded reasonable facilities for rest and sleep, and that he is properly fed. In the event of any member of the force, whether senior in rank or not, attempting to treat the person inhumanely or contrary to Garda Regulations, the Custodial Guardian should forthwith intervene to prevent such abuse. If he considers that such abuse has occurred, he should at once record the relevant facts in the Log-book (referred to in paragraph 50 hereafter) and report the matter to his immediate superior. We so recommend.

49. In the case of a person detained or arrested under the Offences Against the State Act, 1939, or

the Emergency Powers Act, 1976, the Custodial Guardian should be a member of the force of a rank not below that of Inspector, to be assigned by the Chief Superintendent of the Division in which the person is detained. We so recommend.

50. A new Station record, to be known as the Station Log-book, should be devised and supplied immediately to all Garda Stations. The Log-book should be used to record the history of each person arrested and detained from the time of arrest or detention to the time of release or transfer to Court, prison or other authority outside the Station. Every contact with the person in custody should be recorded and initialled by the Custodial Guardian. The ultimate responsibility for the proper maintenance of the Log-book should rest with him. A suggested format for a page in the Log-book is given in Appendix F, but this is offered merely as a suggestion of the type of information which should be recorded. The record should be kept in triplicate; one copy should be forwarded immediately to the Divisional Officer of the Division in which the person is detained; another copy should accompany the arrested party when he is brought in custody out of the Station and should be furnished, where appropriate, to the District Justice before whom the party is remanded; the third copy should be retained in the Station. We so recommend.

51. A 'Central Agency' should be instituted in every Garda District for the recording of the whereabouts of every person taken into custody therein. Immediately upon the arrival of the person of the Garda Station the Central Agency at District Headquarters should be informed. The whereabouts of the person in custody should be made known, upon

request and as of right, to any member of the legal profession or any member of the person's family — the latter only with the permission of the person in custody. We so recommend.

52. A situation may arise where a person is arrested and detained in a District other than that in which he resides. We feel justified in suggesting that a special additional measure be taken to meet the eventuality. In such a case where the Custodial Guardian becomes, or is made aware of the fact, he should notify the whereabouts of the person in custody to both his own District Central Agency and that of the District in which the person resides. We so recommend.

53. If an arrested person indicates desire or willingness to make a voluntary statement, he should be afforded the opportunity of writing out same in his own hand. If he prefers to have the statement taken down by a Garda, a sentence to this effect should be included at the beginning of the written statement. We so recommend.

54. If a person in custody in a Garda Station agrees to answer questions about matters other than the crime for which he is in custody, the interrogation should take place in a room set aside for this purpose. The room should be sufficiently furnished for basic human comfort. Anything suggestive of intimidation, isolation or deprivation should be avoided. We so recommend.

55. If an arrested person has asked for a named solicitor, a reasonable time should elapse to allow for the attendance of the solicitor. The duration of a 'reasonable time' must necessarily depend on circumstances, but we regard a period of not less than one hour and not more than two hours as reasonable in

most cases. Questioning in the absence of the solicitor should not commence until the 'reasonable time' has elapsed. The solicitor should be granted access to his client immediately on arrival at the Station, the consultation to be out of the hearing of the Gardaí but subject to such requirements as to safe custody as may be necessary. The solicitor should be entitled, as of right, to attend any subsequent interrogation as an observer. We so recommend.

56. If a solicitor whose attendance has been requested by an arrested person fails to attend within the 'reasonable time', and the arrested person indicates a willingness to answer questions, questioning may take place. We so recommend.

57. The Custodial Guardian should be entitled to attend throughout questioning of an arrested person, but he should not be entitled to intervene. If he deems it advisable, he should be entitled to call for medical examination at any time. If the doctor is of opinion that questioning, or further questioning, is inadvisable, and so certifies, no questioning should take place. We so recommend.

58. Questioning within the confines of a Garda Station can be a traumatic experience for all but the hardened criminal. It seems appropriate that steps should be taken to draw up regulations governing questioning procedures in those cases where questioning is permissible, as, for example, the Offences Against the State Act, 1939. Such regulations should allow the Gardaí to ask questions in a fair and humane manner, and at the same time protect the person being questioned from feeling isolated, vulnerable or intimidated. We believe that not more than two Gardaí should be entitled to question a prisoner at one time, and that not more than four Gardaí should

be present at any one time. Prolonged questioning should not be permitted; at most, four hours of questioning should be allowed, followed by a break of one hour (or two hours, when the break includes time for eating a meal). Only in exceptional circumstances should questioning take place between the hours of midnight and 8 a.m. e.g. where there may be reason to believe that accomplices are escaping, or evidence is being destroyed. We so recommend.

59. The investigation of complaints by members of the public against the Garda Síochána should be brought into line with more enlightened practice in Western Europe. A complaints Tribunal with a strong independent element should be set up. We do not feel called upon to spell out how its membership should be composed, although the desirability of having an expert penologist and an experienced criminal lawyer suggests itself. Whatever its composition, the membership should be clearly so impartial and above any suggestion of bias that it would earn the respect and co-operation of both Garda Síochána and public. We cannot emphasise too strongly our belief that any such Tribunal must have the wholehearted support of th Gardaí if it is to function effectively, and no effort shuld be spared to secure the goodwill of the several Representative Bodies. Whatever procedure is adopted for dealing with complaints, no suggestion of double jeopardy should arise. We so recommend.

60. On the first occasion an accused appears in the District Court, the Prosecution should be required by the District Justice to say whether any statement or confession made by the accused will be relied upon. If the answer is in the affirmative the Justice should enquire of the accused whether or not such confession or statement was made freely. If the answer is that

147

the confession or statement was not made freely, the accused should be permitted, but not compelled, to elaborate, particularly with regard to any alleged ill-treatment. The proceedings in the District Court should be duly recorded, and the record (including the original of any statement) should later be available to the trial Court. We so recommend.

61. A person who suffers injury while in Garda custody because of ill-treatment by a member or members of the force should be entitled to claim and to receive compensation out of State funds. This right should be maintained even in cases where the offending member or members cannot be identified. We so recommend.

62. The Law Society delegation which appeared before us regarded as feasible a scheme whereby a panel of 'duty solicitors' could be maintained. Solicitors on the panel for any given day would be available to attend at a local Garda Station when a prisoner requests the advice of a solicitor but is unable to name a solicitor of his own. A feasibility study of the subject should be undertaken forthwith. We so recommend.

63. Many Garda Stations are unsuitable for the detention of persons in custody for prolonged periods. In the case of subversive crime a maximum period of 48 hours' detention is possible under the Offences Against the State Act, 1939. Should the Emergency Powers Act, 1976, be reactivated, a maximum period of seven days' detention would become possible. In no case should a person be detained in Garda custody for more than 48 hours; if detention for a longer period is permitted by law, any period in excess of 48 hours should be spent in prison or other convenient place. We so recommend.

64. The forensic facilities available to the Garda Síochána are, by all accounts, seriously inadequate and compare unfavourably with those available to police forces elsewhere. Immediate priority should be given to the development of adequate facilities in this field. Reliance on confessions and self-inculpatory statements should be lessened and the solution of crime by other methods of police-work made possible. We so recommend.

65. The training of Garda recruits and the in-service training of members of the Garda Síochána should lay stress on the proper treatment of persons in Garda custody, having regard to their legal rights as laid down in the United Nations Declaration on Human Rights and other international agreements and conventions. We so recommend.

66. In order to reduce the number of people held in Garda custody, an offender should not be arrested in any case in which he may be made amenable to the law by way of summons. In addition, bail should be granted by the Gardaí under the powers conferred on them by section 31 of the Criminal Procedure Act, 1967, in every case where it is believed that an arrested person will attend Court to answer the charge laid against him, and that he will not interfere with winesses. We so recommend.

67. Feasibility studies should be instituted at once to establish whether videotaping of interrogations in the investigation of serious crime is a viable proposition. In addition, tape-recording should be tried on as wide a basis as possible. It is fully appreciated that a variety of technical and legal difficulties will have to be surmounted, but we believe that a start should be made at once in trying out mechanical aids. Persons being questioned should be informed that the inter-

rogation is being recorded. We so recommend.

68. Consideration should be given to embodying in a comprehensive statute the protection to be afforded to persons in custody, and the powers and duties of the Garda Síochána in dealing with them. We so recommend.

BARRA Ó BRIAIN
Chairman

RUAIDHRI ROBERTS

PATRICK MALONE

G. L. FREWEN B.L.
Secretary

Chairman's Addendum

I am in agreement with my two colleagues save, as mentioned in paragraph 44, in regard to the interpretation of the Committee's Terms of Reference with respect to the matter of detention for the purpose of interrogation and the matter of the right of silence.

The argument that these matters were both outside the Terms of Reference was put forward by only one group of all those who attended before us. The others, for the most part, assumed without question that these matters might properly be discussed and considered by the Committee. The Law Society, having specifically considered the question at our request, were of opinion that neither was outside the Terms of Reference. This too is my own considered opinion. Accordingly I feel that I should go somewhat further than my two colleagues and make recommendations in regard to both of these matters in addition to those recommended by all three members in our joint report.

I cannot ignore the fact that, in several other countries having, like Ireland, a Common Law Jurisprudence, these two questions have been considered and debated over a long period by Commissions of the highest standing whose conclusions, and the reasons for same, have been published and made available to us. Furthermore, eminent judges in the United Kingdom and in the United States of America and several Professors of Law have expressed their views on the need for changes in the law in regard to both detention for custodial interrogation and the right of silence.

In the much discussed case of *Miranda v. State of*

Arizona 384 U.S. 436 (1966) in the Supreme Court of the United States, Mr. Justice Harlan, with whom Mr. Justice Stewart and Mr. Justice White joined, dissenting, used these words, with which I entirely agree: 'Those who use third-degree tactics and deny them in court are equally able and destined to lie as skilfully about warnings and waivers'. I can think of no way of guaranteeing that ill-treatment of persons in Garda custody will not take place except by providing, as far as practicable, the surveillance of an independent eye-witness throughout that custody. Whilst I share my colleagues' views on this matter, I would go somewhat further and question whether or not the time has now come to change the law relating to the investigation of crime by providing a form of 'detention' for a strictly limited period. During such detention the Gardaí would have the right to hold persons *reasonably suspected of having committed a crime*, but only such persons, for the express purpose of questioning them in relation to the crime. The Gardaí lack such power at the moment. Notwithstanding this, they are under extreme and increasing pressure from the whole community which is clamant that the police uncover and prevent crime and bring guilt home to guilty parties. Is it any wonder that the allegations which we have considered show a picture, again and again, of the Gardaí frustrated by their lack of legal power to question suspected persons in custody, taking the law into their own hands by holding them for custodial interrogation, and in doing so, breaking the law if not indeed the Constitution.' This is so even apart from ill-treatment. But the allegations we have considered state that in a number of cases the Gardaí in their frustration have used physical violence or threats of violence to secure answers to their questioning. If, therefore, this element of frustration can be eliminated, or even reduced, in some cases, by a change of the law, it seems to me that this change would afford per se some further safeguard against ill-treatment. But the change cannot be made by the Gardaí or even by the Judges. It is, in my view, strictly and clearly a matter for the Oireachtas.

The same difficulties have arisen in other countries having a Common Law system of jurisprudence where it is recognised and admitted that the same irregularities consistently take place. In Scotland, the question has been considered by Lord Thomson's Committee on Criminal Procedure in Scotland (Second Report Cmnd 6218), and in Australia by the Commonwealth Law Reform Commission (Report No. 2). Both of these bodies favoured a new legal concept of a period of 'detention' or 'restraint' as distinct from formal 'arrest'. During a period of 'detention or restraint' the police would have the right to question a person in custody closely but always in a fair manner. In Scotland the period recommended was six hours. In Australia the period suggested was four hours, extendable in certain cases. I would favour the amendment of the law here to provide that *a person reasonably suspected of crime* but none others might be 'detained' for questioning until the Gardaí either decide to arrest and charge him formally, or alternatively to release him, but, in no case, for longer than a period of six hours.

It is both logic and common sense that a person investigating a matter should question those concerned in the subject under investigation, check their answers and if there are apparent discrepancies, come back to the person questioned for an explanation.

The police work on suspicion and hearsay and on many other factors which are not legal evidence. The Courts, on the other hand, proceed entirely upon legal evidence. The 'detention' period would give the Gardaí an interval during which to do what is strictly police work. The law at present largely denies this to the Gardaí. The suspect should, of course, be told the charge in relation to which he is being detained. Furthermore, all that happens to him while detained at the Garda Station (visits by legal adviser, doctor, relatives, etc) should be carefully logged in the officially prescribed Station record.

This power to 'detain' in order to question is already provided for in the Offences Against the State Act, 1939, and I would recommend that the six hours mentioned above be adopted as the norm in all cases, with certain powers for a District Justice or a Peace Commissioner to extend the normal period for a strictly limited time in respect of cases covered by that Act and the Emergency Powers Act, 1976, rather than the lengthy periods now set out in these two Acts.

A second matter, related to the foregoing, is whether or not a suspect should continue to have the absolute right to remain silent in all cases. At present, thre is no legal obligation to give information to the Gardaí, apart from certain statutory exceptions. No adverse inference may be drawn by any jury from such silence. The Prosecution may not even comment on it. This rule as it stands has been criticised by several very distinguished judges in England, and by well-known teachers of law and authors. In England in June, 1972, the Criminal Law Revision Committee, after considering the matter for eight years, advocated the abolition of the right of silence as it hitherto existed. The British section of the International Commission of Jurists chaired by Sir John Foster Q.C., M.P., was of opinion that the privilege of the accused to keep silent before his trial should be abolished. The Lord Chief Justice of England, Lord Widgery, has expressed the view that the right to remain silent should be modified. So has Professor Rupert Cross of Oxford University. Professor Glanville Williams has expressed the view that changes in the law must include the abandonment of the present entitlement of a suspected or accused person to take no part whatsoever in the establishment of the truth. This right of silence can be no less frustrating to Gardaí, honestly and dutifully investigating a crime, than the probhibition on holding suspects for the purpose of questioning them. Like risks of ill-treatment of persons in custody are involved. I would favour lessening this risk of ill-treatment in the interests of both suspects and Gardaí. I consider that this rule of law should be somewhat modified and that a suspect should be required to answer certain questions. A refusal or failure to do so might be made the subject of comment by the judge at the trial and/or by the Prosecution with the leave of the trial judge. The jury should be told to draw what inference they think proper and commonsense from a refusal to answer all or any such question. Such questions might relate to identity and address, marital status, explanation of stains on clothing, property (including money) found upon the suspect, an account of his dealings with a vehicle believed by the Gardaí to have been used in a crime, his movements for a specified period of time before and after the crime, and some other kindred questions to be set out in a statute and strictly limited. Outside of such matters the suspected person would retain his right of silence, as at present, quite unimpaired.

BARRA Ó BRIAIN

Appendices

APPENDIX A

Organisations and persons specifically invited by letter to make submissions to the Committee:

The Bar Council
The Law Society
Amnesty International
Irish Association of Civil Liberty
Irish Council for Civil Liberties
Prisoners' Rights Organisation
The Commissioner of the Garda Síochána
Representative Body for Chief Superintendents
Representative Body for Superintendents
Representative Body for Inspectors, Station Sergeants
    and Sergeants
Representative Body for Guards

APPENDIX B

Organisations and persons who made written submissions:

The Bar Council
The Law Society
Amnesty International
Irish Association of Civil Liberty

The Commissioner of the Garda Síochána
Representative Body for Chief Superintendents
Representative Body for Inspectors, Station Sergeants
and Sergeants
Representative Body for Guards
The Irish Commission for Justice and Peace
Messrs. Dudley Potter, Donnchadh Lehane, Garrett
Sheehan, Brain Gallagher, Pol Ó Murchu, Con
Lehane and Myles P. Shevlin, Solicitors
Mr. John Glynn, Solicitor
Mr. Joseph Killilea, 12 Kirkpatrick Ave., Clonsilla, Co.
Dublin
An t-Uasal Liam Ó Dulachain, 15 Bothar Ghrainseach
an Dein, An Charriag Dhubh, Contae Átha Cliath
Mr. Desmond J. McCabe, Verdun, Glenageary, Co.
Dublin
Superintendent F. T. Murphy, Disciplinary Investigat-
ing Officer Dublin Metropolitan Area
Mr. Robert Pierse, Solicitor
Professor Kevin Boyle, Faculty of Law, University
College, Galway.

APPENDIX C

Organisations or groups which were invited to
make oral submissions to enlarge on the written submissions already furnished:

The Bar Council
The Law Society
Amnesty International
Irish Association of Civil Liberty
The Commissioner of the Garda Síochána
Representative Body for Chief Superintendents

Representative Body for Superintendents
Representative Body for Inspectors, Station Sergeants and Sergeants
Representative Body for Guards
The Irish Commission for Justice and Peace
Messrs. Dudley Potter, Donnchadh Lehane, Garrett Sheehan, Brian Gallagher, Pol Ó Murchu, Con Lehane and Myles P. Shevlin, Solicitors.

APPENDIX D

THE JUDGES' RULES

1. When a police officer is endeavouring to discover the author of a crime there is no objection to his putting questions in respect thereof to any person or persons, whether suspected or not, from whom he thinks that useful information may be obtained.
2. Whenever a police officer has made up his mind to charge a person with a crime, he should first caution such person before asking him any questions, or any further questions as the case may be.
3. Persons in custody should not be questioned without the usual caution being first administered.
4. If the prisoner wishes to volunteer any statement, the usual caution should be administered. It is desirable that the last two words of such caution should be omitted, and that the caution should end with the words 'be given in evidence'.
5. The caution to be administered to a prisoner when he is formally charged should therefore be in the following words: 'Do you wish to say any-

thing in answer to the charge? You are not obliged to say anything unless you wish to do so, but whatever you say will be taken down in writing and may be given in evidence'. Care should be taken to avoid the suggestion that his answers can only be used in evidence against him, as this may prevent an innocent person making a statement which might assist to clear him of the charge.

6. A statement made by a prisoner before there is time to caution him is not rendered inadmissible in evidence merely because no caution has been given, but in such a case he should be cautioned as soon as possible.

7. A prisoner making a voluntary statement must not be cross-examined, and no questions should be put to him about it except for the purpose of removing ambiguity in what he has actually said. For instance, if he has mentioned an hour without saying whether it was morning or evening, or has given a day of the week and day of the month which do not agree, or has not made it clear to what individual or what place be intended to refer in some part of his statement, he may be questioned sufficiently to clear up the point.

8. When two or more persons are charged with the same offence and their statements are taken separately, the police should not read these statements to the other persons charged, but each of such persons should be given by the police a copy of such statements and nothing should be said or done by the police to invite a reply. If the person charged desires to make a statement in reply the usual caution should be administered.

9. Any statement made in accordance with the above rules should, whenever possible, be taken

down in writing and signed by the person making it after it has been read to him and he has been invited to make any corrections he may wish.

APPENDIX E

C. 72 (S).

GARDA SÍOCHÁNA

INFORMATION FOR PERSONS IN CUSTODY

BAIL
The Sergeant or member in charge of a Garda Station may release on bail a person who is brought in custody to the Garda Station if that member considers it prudent to do so and no warrant directing the detention of that person is in force. If the person is not released on bail by the sergeant or member in charge, he or she may apply for bail on appearing at a court before a District Justice or a Peace Commissioner.

FACILITIES
Provided it is reasonable and practicable, the following facilities will be afforded to a person in custody in a Garda Station:—

(1) A Solicitor, a member of the person's family or a friend will, by arrangement with the sergeant or member in charge of the station, be contacted and informed that the person has been taken into custody.
(2) The person may receive a visit from and consult privately with a Solicitor.

(3) The person may receive a visit from a member of his or her family or a friend, provided that such visit is not considered prejudicial to the interests of justice and is supervised by a member of the Garda Síochána.

REFRESHMENTS
Refreshments are supplied free of charge to persons in custody. If, however, a person wishes to procure a meal of his or her choice, arrangements will be made to have a meal supplied at his or her own expense, if this is practicable.

LEGAL AID
This is dealt with on application to the court and may be granted in certain circumstances.

FINGERPRINTS
Under the Offences Against the State Act, 1939, a member of the Garda Síochána is authorised to take, or cause to be taken, the fingerprints of any person arrested under Section 30 of that Act. In any other case, a member of the Garda Síochána may take the fingerprints of a person in custody in a Garda Station, with his or her consent.

IDENTIFICATION PARADES
A person whom it is proposed to put on parade should be informed:

(1) that the person will be placed among a number of other persons who are, as far as possible, of similar height, age and general appearance as the person;
(2) that the person may have a Solicitor or a friend present at the parade;

(3) that the person may take up any position he or she may choose in the parade and that, after a witness has left, he or she may change his or her position in the parade if he or she so wishes before the next witness is called;

(4) that the person may object to any of the persons on the parade or the arrangements and that any such objection should be made to the member conducting the parade.

APPENDIX F

AN GARDA SÍOCHÁNA   Form X

Garda Station at . . . .   Prisoner No . . . .

Section A

1. Name of person in custody . . . .
2. Address of same. . . . .
3. Name number and rank of arresting member . . . .
4. Date and time of arrest as given by arresting member . . . .
5. Date and time of arrival at Garda Station . . . .
6. Reason (in brief) for detention . . . .
7. Name, number and rank of Custodial Guardian . . . .
8. Whether prisoner's condition normal   Yes . . . No . . .
9. If condition abnormal give brief details . . . .
10. Did prisoner make any complaint on arrival at Station? . . . .
11. If so, give brief details . . . .
12. Was medical examination sought on arrival by
    (a) prisoner . . . .
    (b) Custodial Guardian . . . .
13. Whereabouts of prison notirfied to District HQ at . . . . . . hours

Section B

1. Printed Notice of Rights handed to prisoner by . . . .
   at . . . . hours
2. Did prisoner ask for attendance of (a) legal adviser? . . . .
                                        (b) member of family? . . . . .
                                        (c) friend? . . . .
                                        (d) doctor? . . . .

3. If so, furnish name(s) and address(es) of person(s) sought
   ....
   ....
4. Give details of efforts made to contact person(s) sought
   ....
5. Details of all persons coming into contact with prisoner

Name	Rank or relationship	Purpose of visit	Date and Time	
			In	Out

6. Prisoner visited by Custodial Guardian

Time	Remarks

Section C

1. Date and time of prisoner's release . . . .
   or prisoner's removal from Station . . . .
   or change of responsibility for Custodial Guardianship. . . . .
2. Reason for same. . . . .
3. Signature of prisoner on release . . . .
   or Garda removing prisoner from Station . . . .
   or New Custodial Guardian . . . .
4. Countersignature of Old Custodial Guardian . . . .
5. If condition of prisoner has altered, or if complaint made by
   prisoner, give details . . . .
6. Information as to prisoner's whereabouts notified to District HQ
   at . . . . hours by . . . .

PART III
CAPITAL PUNISHMENT

The Right To Take Life: Is Capital Punishment Justified?
Father Austin Flannery, OP

Some thirty years ago, Mr Seán MacBride said in Dáil Éireann that it was 'probably no exaggeration to say that the concept of capital punishment had its origin in barbarism'. That was on 21 November 1951, three years before the last execution had taken place in the Republic of Ireland and thirteen years before the — almost, but not quite — total abolition of capital punishment in the Republic. The death penalty was retained for treason, some military offences and four types of murder: (a) murder of a garda acting in the course of his/her duty, (b) murder of a prison officer in the course of his/her duty, (c) murder for a political motive of the head of a foreign state, or a member of the government or diplomatic officer of a foreign state, (d) murder done in the course of an offence under certain sections of the 1939 Offences Against the State Act, or in furtherance of the activities of an unlawful organisation (within the meaning of section 18 of that Act.)

Distinguished lawyer that he is, Mr MacBride did not then and does not now use words lightly. The word 'barbarism' on his lips merits attention, especially in view of the consideration that it is likely that not many people, and not even all of those who favour the total abolition of the death penalty, would see it as barbaric. As the Amnesty International Report, 'The Death Penalty,' puts it (p. 17):

> 'Widespread concern about the use of the death penalty as a matter of principle is felt only in a minority of countries. In most of the world, the death penalty is not a public issue and there is little to suggest that many societies regard putting someone to death after judicial process as abhorrent. Governments tend to justify the use of the death penalty on the ground that public opinion is in favour of it for certain crimes. They do not, in general, offer proof that the death penalty has validity as a deterrent: they simply reiterate the statement that it has.'

That report was issued in 1979; in 1977 Amnesty International had convened an international conference at Stockholm on capital punishment. One of the papers prepared for the delegates to the conference, 'Capital Punishment, Public Opinion and the Mass Media', by Marcel Berline, had this to say:

> 'Religious bodies play less of a part in the debate on capital punishment than might be expected of institutions of such enormous potential influence over so many millions of people. The Catholic Church and most other Christian churches with a substantial following do not take a firm stand either way on the issue. Nor does Buddhism. They are not opposed to judicial execution as such in principle and are usually content to leave decisions on whom to execute to the temporal power, intervening only to the extent of calling for mercy to be extended in particular cases. Neither the western churches nor the eastern

religions adopt any blanket opposition to capital punishment and it is left to some of the smaller, less influential religions and religious bodies to carry the torch of abolition.'

In fact, since the above was written, influential Christian voices have been raised in favour of the abolition of the death penalty, amongst them the Roman Catholic hierarchies of France, the United States and Ireland. In the meantime, it seems to me that it is important to highlight the barbarity of the death penalty, as does Amnesty International, for example, in its report. It says: 'Execution by whatever means and for whatever offence is a cruel, inhuman and degrading punishment' (p. 3), re-echoing the United Nations Declaration of Human Rights: 'Nobody shall be subjected to torture or to cruel, inhuman or degrading treatment or punishment.' The book carries gruesome photographs of the death-dealing apparatus in common use in judicial killings, as well as photographs of victims of hangings, including public hangings, and of firing-squads.

It can be objected that this is an emotive approach to a delicate and complex problem, an approach calculated to provoke an emotional response, thus lessening the possibility of wise decision-making. Comparable statistics and photographs of the bodies of murderers' victims could equally well trigger off a demand for the retention or the re-introduction of the death penalty, it can be reasonably urged. An even more powerful emotional stimulus to a demand for the retention of capital punishment, or its re-introduction, is alarm and concern over the spread of violence, especially terrorist violence. This would seem to have happened in the United States in the late seventies, where there was extended public debate regarding the necessity and advisability of retaining the death penalty. The United States bishops, in their 'Statement on Capital Punishment' (text in *Origins*, 27 Nov. 1980) wrote:

> 'We should note that much of this debate was carried on in a time of intense public concern about crime and violence. For instance, in 1976 alone more than 18,000 people were murdered in the United States.'

The Commission for Justice and Peace of the Irish Roman Catholic Bishops put this figure in perspective for Irish readers by remarking that it would be 'equivalent to a murder rate of about 250 per year in the Republic of Ireland. This compares with the actual Irish rate of 19 in that year.' ('For the Abolition of Capital Punishment.')

I would argue that abolitionists are justified if they try to make the public vividly aware of the barbarity of the death penalty, even if this leaves them open to the accusation of an emotive approach. If retentionists, on the other hand, focus attention on the barbarity of murder as an argument for the death penalty, they are advocating the duplication of that same barbarity by the State. This is not so much inconsistency (though inconsistency there certainly is) as very primitive morality: an eye for an eye. The Irish Bishops' Commission for Justice and Peace was being both more consistent and more Christian when it urged, in 1976, that 'no one could in conscience ask the State to abolish the death penalty if he or she encouraged or condoned directly or indirectly, by action or sentiment, the use of violence against the person by anyone else in Ireland,

170

for whatever reason.' (Quoted in 'For the Abolition of Capital Punishment').

Arthur Koestler, one of the most forceful proponents of the abolition of capital punishment, put his case in 'Reflections on Hanging,' which has been described by the eminent English sociologist, Professor James Halloran, as 'quite obviously emotional' ('Capital Punishment: A Case for Abolition', by M. Tidmarsh, J. D. Halloran and K. J. Connolly, London, 1963). Another British abolitionist wrote of Koestler's book that 'it may well be seen that . . . [it] helped to change the course of our social history and completed the process of a century or more during which capital punishment in Britain had been under constant sentence.' (J. A. Joyce, 'The Right to Life — A World View of Capital Punishment', London, 1962, p. 103)

The reason for bringing home to people the barbarity of the death penalty is that it is something exacted on their behalf and in their name, and most obviously so in a democracy. The individual citizen cannot be held responsible for any and every murder, whatever might be said about his or her share of responsibility for the inequalities and deprivations which are the breeding-ground for *some* crimes and for *some* murders. But individual citizens cannot altogether divest themselves of responsibility for the death penalty, where it is still exacted. They may not particularly want it, they may be against it, but if this is so they must find ways and means of making this clear. Professor J. T. Sellin of the USA has been described (by James Halloran, op. cit. p. 44) as the 'world's greatest authority on the statistics relating to capital punishment'. In his evidence to the British Royal Commission on Capital Punishment,

1949-53, he stated that:

> 'the question of whether the death penalty is to
> be dropped, retained or instituted is not dependent
> on evidence as to its utilitarian effects, but on the
> strength of popular beliefs and sentiments not
> easily influenced by such evidence. These beliefs
> and sentiments have their roots in a people's
> culture. They are conditioned by a multitude
> of factors, such as the character of social insti-
> tutions, social, economic and political ideas. When
> a people no longer *likes* the death penalty for
> murders it will be removed no matter what may
> happen to the homicide rate.' (Halloran, op. cit.,
> p. 44)

I have come across another approach to the problem, one which examined the attitudes and motivation of supporters of capital punishment. I have
read a lengthy essay by two American sociologists
which offered a very unflattering pen-portrait, the
result of their researches, of a typical supporter of
capital punishment. I have listened to equally unflattering descriptions, of an unscientific character
be it said, of opponents of capital punishment.
Such an approach has a certain fascination, certainly, but more important is the need to examine the
problem dispassionately and objectively. And just
as essential as influencing public opinion.

Capital punishment was once a very common
punishment, meted out for a large number of crimes.
'In England, for example, during the 18th century,
death was decreed for several hundred specific offences, particularly for those against property' (*Encyclopaedia Brittanica*). To remedy that situation, Samuel
Romilly began in 1808 asking Parliament to abolish

172

the death penalty for certain crimes. Offences which carried the death penalty included: stealing goods to the value of 40s or more in a private dwelling-house, or to the value of 5s or more in a shop, defacing Westminster Bridge and consorting with gipsies. Gerard Gardiner ('Capital Punishment as a Deterrent: And the Alternative', London, p. 24) relates that thirteen people were hanged for this latter offence at one assize.

Romilly had little enough success in his campaign. Such bills as he managed to get through the House of Commons were invariably thrown out by the House of Lords, where they encountered powerful opposition from the judicial members. Halloran (op. cit., p. 48) quotes the Chief Justice for 1810 on a Private Stealing Bill:

'If we suffer this Bill to pass we shall not know where we stand — we shall not know whether we are upon our heads or our feet... Repeal this law and see the contrast — no man can trust himself for an hour out of doors without the most alarming apprehensions that on his return every vestige of his property will be swept off by the hardened robber.'

Interestingly, Mr MacBride quoted the above passage in Dáil Éireann in 1951 during a debate on capital punishment.

The argument that capital punishment has an uniquely deterrent value is still heard today, but more than once even in the last century the Commissioners of the Criminal Law in England expressed the contrary opinion. In 1886, fifteen years after the death penalty had been confined to four offences in Britain (high treason, murder, piracy with violence and the

173

destruction of public arsenals and dockyards) the Commissioners of the Criminal Law stated in their report: 'It has not in effect been found that the repeal of capital punishment with regard to any particular class of offences has been attended with an increase of offenders.' (Halloran, p. 49).

A highly significant statistic from the last century in Britain relates to public execution. Those who argue that executions have an uniquely deterrent effect must surely accept that they ought to be much more effective if done in public. Yet evidence was placed before the Royal Commission of 1866 that of 167 persons who had been sentenced to death in one town over a number of years, 164 had themselves witnessed a public execution. It was because of this evidence that public executions were discontinued. Halloran (op. cit., p. 50) comments drily:

'It is perhaps not surprising that the commission concluded that the judges could not be right in the view which they had expressed in favour of the continuance of public executions on the grounds of their special quality as a deterrent.'

In listing the arguments for and against capital punishment, the Encyclopaedia Britannica puts the argument in favour of capital punishment as follows:

'that it deters people from committing crime; life imprisonment, it is said, would not be equally effective as a deterrent and would expose prison staffs and fellow prisoners to dangerous murderers. This risk later extends to the community, as such persons may escape, or be pardoned or paroled.'

Amnesty International's Report, in listing the arguments in favour of capital punishment, adds to the above the argument that 'for particularly reprehensible crimes, death is the only fitting and adequate punishment.' It also makes more explicit the point made in the last sentence quoted above, when it recounts the argument: 'Those who commit certain grave offences must be put to death for the protection of society at large.'

These arguments coincide with two of the justifications traditionally advanced for punishment — retribution and deterrence. Deterrence is intended to contribute to the protection of society. If you deter criminals from committing crime you have protected society. The question remains whether killing a criminal is the *only* way of deterring him or her from further criminal activity, and whether it is the most effective way — or indeed the uniquely effective way — of deterring others.

I accept that, to quote the American Bishops' 'Statement on Capital Punishment': 'Punishment, since it involves the deliberate infliction of evil on another, is always in need of justification.' The upholders of capital punishment must therefore prove their case. The *onus probandi* rests with them. And (even though I am being repetitious) they need to prove not merely that capital punishment effectively deters others from crime — I accept that it deters the convicted criminal, but so does imprisonment! They need to prove that capital punishment, in the words of the Irish Commission for Justice and Peace, 'will clearly deter other potential criminals and that it is significantly superior to any other available means.'

The following considerations lend considerable weight to the argument that it is for the upholders of capital punishment to offer clear proof that capital punishment is an uniquely effective deterrent:

(1) There is nowadays, in the words of the Irish Commission for Justice and Peace, 'a growing awareness of the intrinsic sacredness of all human life'. Or, as Mr Ramsey Clark puts it ('Crime in America') 'Surely the abolition of the death penalty is a major milestone in the long road up from barbarism.... There is no justification for the death penalty. It demeans life. Its inhumanity raises basic questions about our institutions and our purpose as a people. Why must we kill? What do we fear?' (pp. 336-337). One would, of course, do all in one's power to spread an awareness of the sacredness of human life throughout the whole of society. But if some individuals do not want to hear, does one put matters right by killing them? As if there were no chance of correction, reform, rehabilitation?

(2) Miscarriage of justice can and does occur. Mr Ramsey Clark narrates that 'Because the death penalty is irrevocable, Lafayette vowed to oppose it until "the infallibility of human judgment was demonstrated to him."' Mr Clark went on: 'Innocent persons have been executed. In addition, some incapable of knowing what they did — the mentally retarded and the disturbed — have been [executed].' (pp. 334-335). To be effective, the judicial process depends on the reliability of witnesses, the efficiency of police, the skill and the knowledge of lawyers, the judgment of jurors and the wisdom of judges — to say nothing of veracity, integrity, freedom from prejudice and corruption in all of them, all of these qualities being among the most delicate of the plants to grow in the human psyche. It would be difficult to disagree with the opinion expressed by the American Catholic Bishops: '... the possibility of mistake cannot be eliminated

from the system.' A mistake which cannot be subsequently rectified.

(3) The system works in haphazard fashion. Ramsey Clark writes: 'A small group of offenders selected by chance have been destroyed. Most who committed similar crimes were never caught. Nearly all of the persons caught and convicted of the same crimes for which a few were killed have been imprisoned — not executed.' (p. 335)

(4) A poor person sta ds a better chance of conviction than a well-off person, for the simple reason that the well-to-do person can afford the best legal aid, to say nothing of whatever class or racial prejudices may operate to the detriment of the poorer person. Some startling statistics from the United States bear this out. Ramsey Clark writes: 'Since we began keeping records in 1930, there have been 2,066 negroes and only 1,715 white persons put to death. Negroes have been only one-eighth of our population. Hundreds of thousands of rapes have occurred in America since 1930, yet only 455 men have been executed for rape — and 405 of them were negroes.' (p. 335) The American bishops note ' . . . those condemned to die are nearly always poor and are disproportionately black. Thus 47 per cent of the inmates on Death Row are black, whereas only 11 per cent of the American population is black.'

(5) Delay, pending appeals, between conviction and execution and the methods of execution create anguish for those convicted and for their relatives and friends, as well as occasioning great distress for witnesses and for the other prisoners.

(6) In the words of the Irish Commission for Justice and Peace, 'In Ireland, most murders are "one-off" murders, the sort which, in the words of the United

States Catholic Conference, are rarely undertaken "in a spirit of rational calculation" which would be influenced by a remote threat of death.'

(7) It has been often observed that the only genuinely effective deterrent is, to quote the Irish Commission for Justice and Peace, 'a high rate of detection, conviction and imprisonment.'

However, it would appear that empirical studies which have been carried out do not in the least justify the claim that capital punishment is a deterrent, and an uniquely effective deterrent. The American bishops note: 'Empirical studies in this area have not given conclusive evidence that would justify the imposition of the death penalty on a few individuals as a means of preventing others from committing crimes.' And the Irish Commission for Justice and Peace concludes: ' . . . the most that can be said about the effects of capital punishment is that, while it cannot be conclusively demonstrated to have no deterrent effect, studies have generally failed to establish any meaningful correlation between the death penalty and the rate of serious criminality.'

Index

183

Index compiled by Helen Litton

AMNESTY INTERNATIONAL

IRISH SECTION

AMNESTY INTERNATIONAL WORKS

* for men and women imprisoned for their beliefs in crowded jails and remote labour camps throughout the world,

* for thousands of political prisoners denied any possibility of a just trial,

* for the many subjected to torture,

* for the abolition of the death penalty,

* and for an end to the practise of abductions and "disappearances" carried out by a number of governments against their own citizens.

IT NEEDS YOUR SUPPORT!

Send applications for membership or donations to:

AMNESTY INTERNATIONAL,
8th Floor,
Liberty Hall
Dublin 1.
Telephone (01) 728800

International Peace Bureau

Founded in 1892. Nobel Peace Prize 1910. Consultative Status with the United Nations.

"The taproot of violence in our society today is our intent to use nuclear weapons. Once we have agreed to that, all other evil is minor in comparison. Until we squarely face the question of our consent to use nuclear weapons, any hope of large scale improvement of public morality is doomed to failure".

Richard T. McSorely, S.J.

President:	Seán MacBride
Vice Presidents:	Lord Philip Noel-Baker (Britain)
	Dr Jules Moch (France)
	Mrs Alva Myrdal (Sweden)
	Professor Paul Levy (Belgium)
	Venerable Gyotsu N Sato (Japan, Chairman of the Executive)
Offices:	41 rue de Zurich, CH-1201 Geneva, Switzerland
Telephone:	(022) 31.64.29; Cables: Peacebureau, Geneva